'As a leader in a high-growth, rapidly evolving company it is critical to ensure that everyone is aligned. In this environment hard conversations are inevitable. The tools in this book have lifted the performance of our executive team and our company. If you are dealing with change or growth in your organisation, Mark Rosenberg provides the wisdom and frameworks to help manage that change.'

Dr Rob Newman, CEO, Nearmap Ltd

'Mark Rosenberg has created a readable, concise, and authoritative summary of a universal human challenge: how to have constructive conversations with people with whom one is interdependent yet beset by conflict. As a reader, I felt I was receiving sage advice from a trusted friend.'

Dan Dana, PhD, founder of Mediation Training Institute
at Eckerd College (Florida, US)

First published in 2022 by Mark Rosenberg

A catalogue entry for this book is available from the National Library of Australia.

ISBN: 978-1-922553-86-7

Printed in Australia by McPherson's Printing
Project management and text design by Publish Central
Cover design by Pipeline Design

The paper this book is printed on is certified as environmentally friendly

Disclaimer

Contents

Introduction

You could spend a lifetime trying to understand workplace conflict. World-renowned English cognitive psychologist Michael Kirton did just that. He died in 2020 at the age of 94, having spent a sizeable chunk of his life trying to solve the puzzle of how to increase collaboration and reduce conflict within groups. Kirton identified something that, while obvious, was an epiphany for me in my work with leaders and their teams. He noted that when people work together, two problems always come into play – what he referred to as Problem A and Problem B.

Problem A relates to the task or challenge you are trying to resolve – putting a man on the moon, for example, or rescuing kids trapped in a cave. Problem B relates to how we manage each other – how you manage the relationships with the people you are working with. Ideally, we want to spend the bulk of our time working on Problem A, resolving the substantive issue. However, we often spend more time on Problem B. Our inability to manage relationships gets in the way of doing the substantive work.[1]

This book will help you become better at dealing with Problem B. It will help you manage relationships in the workplace. The practical framework provided and tips on how to navigate conflict will make your life easier and help build your reputation as a leader.

WHY I WROTE THIS BOOK

Like Michael Kirton, I've spent a lot my career working on Problem B. I started my working life as a lawyer, often dealing with hardcore disputes that were expensive and involved a lot of management time. Along the way, I shifted from being a lawyer to a manager, working in both the private and public sector, and soon discovered that conflict wasn't limited to lawyers. Too much of my time was taken up navigating disputes, and this often felt a distraction from the main game. Problem B was real.

My early training as a mediator gave me the skills to navigate the conflict that came along. Dealing with conflict was a strength that I leveraged, and it became an important part of my practice when I started my coaching and mediation business in 2008. Since then, I've helped thousands of leaders become better at having hard conversations. Some of my experiences with these leaders are included in this book (all names have been changed). This book shares my practical approach to conflict management that will improve the way you lead and influence others, no matter your management level.

MY MESSAGE

My key message in this book is this: conflict in the workplace is inevitable. As a leader – whether that be as CEO or part of senior management, or a leader within your team or thought leader within your organisation – being skilled in dealing with conflict and having uncomfortable conversations has enormous benefits. My clients tell me that by improving their skills they have increased their credibility and improved organisational performance.

This book provides a proven, practical, structured approach to help you become a better leader by improving your communication and conflict management skills.

WHAT'S COMING UP

I start by clarifying what I mean by 'hard' conversations. I break down why they are hard and what makes it so important to have them. Then I get into the meaty stuff: how to master the hard conversation. You will gain more understanding of your current approach to conflict management, and what might be holding you back. You'll then learn how to glide through the most challenging of situations by:

- using my practical hard conversations framework
- developing six key communication skills
- working through two powerful case studies that show how the process works.

I also provide an in-depth look at feedback – when to give it, when to hold back, how to do it effectively and how to get better at receiving it.

Finally, I look at how you can manage that small percentage of people who are not merely difficult but almost impossible to deal with – people who even the most skilled, practised and educated communicators struggle with.

Let's get started.

CHAPTER 1

What are hard conversations – and why should you have them?

Imagine a world where the people you work with talk about you as insightful, fair and reasonable, and as an outstanding leader who is not afraid to have the tough conversations. They talk about you as someone who owns their mistakes and has the best interests of the business at heart. They talk about you as someone who is willing to listen and asks great questions.

It's a world where you go into hard conversations feeling nervous, but confident – because you have prepared properly and developed clarity around your objectives and key messages. You anticipate most objections that will be raised and have a plan for how you will respond. You know you might get a curveball or two, but are confident you'll be able to deal with them.

You lead the best team you've ever led. They are aligned and motivated. Your engagement scores are through the roof. Team members feel psychologically safe and will often have healthy debate and conflict. The team make good decisions and deliver outstanding results.

Think about how much less stressed you'd be working in this kind of environment, and how pleased you would be to spend most of your working time on substantive business issues, rather than managing unproductive conflict.

This can be your future. If you want this sort of reality, you need to start having hard conversations.

HARD CONVERSATIONS DEFINED

But what exactly are Hard Conversations?

I define hard conversations as the conversations that you find uncomfortable, awkward, or difficult. They're the conversations that you put off or avoid. You can think about hard conversations as being on a continuum, ranging from scenarios that are mildly uncomfortable, such as having to tell someone their zipper is undone, to situations that are just brutally tough, such as having to tell someone they are being made redundant.

No doubt you have your own experiences of hard conversations at work (or how you avoided them). This book is about helping you become a better leader by becoming more capable and more comfortable having hard conversations. In this chapter, I flesh out the spectrum of hard conversations, explore what makes them hard and discuss why you should have them.

COMMON HARD CONVERSATIONS

Over ten years ago I began running my *Mastering Hard Conversations program* for one of my clients. The program seemed to meet an important need and I've now had more than 2000 people from numerous clients participate. Most of the attendees choose to come to the program (as opposed to being told to come) and it is interesting to understand what drives them to attend. At the start of the program, I say to them, 'Let's try to clarify what we mean when we talk about hard conversations. What scenarios are you experiencing that have drawn you to this program? What hard conversations have you had in the past or are you currently experiencing?'

Table 1.1 shows a summary of these responses, which are broad and varied. Take the time to look through and identify the situations you have experienced. I suspect you will identify quite a few.

Table 1.1: Common hard conversation scenarios at work

Type of management required	Example situations
Managing up: Talking to your direct manager or people with more structural power than you	• Admitting I have made a mistake • Asking for a salary increase • Calling my boss out for poor behaviour • Dealing with a bully manager • Dealing with my manager's assistant (who seems to think they are my boss) • Disagreeing with my manager (who really does not like being challenged) • Having my performance evaluation • Managing a difficult internal customer who has a lot of power • Presenting to the board • Saying no to senior management • Seeking to negotiate additional resources for my team • Telling my boss they are not managing me in a way that is going to get the best out of me • Telling my boss that we don't have the capacity or resources to do what they are asking us to do • Telling my manager (and/or their manager) news that they did not want to hear • Telling my boss I am going to resign

Managing across: Talking to peers and/ or people with similar organisational power	• Admitting I have made a mistake or was wrong • Arguing for my position in face of strong disagreement from others • Calling peers out for poor behaviour or poor performance • Dealing with 'difficult' internal clients/ colleagues in other teams • Dealing with a colleague who is bullying me or other members of our team • Disagreeing with the team's preferred approach • Saying no • Talking to a colleague who keeps interrupting and talking over me • Telling a colleague on our team that they are not pulling their weight • Telling a peer that I disagree with their argument and position • Telling someone their hygiene practices are a problem (for example, they smell bad)
Managing down: Talking to team members who report to you or other people who have less positional power	• Admitting I have made a mistake or was wrong • Calling out direct reports for poor behaviour • Dealing with a direct report who is undermining the team • Giving a performance review where performance is an issue • Giving someone a formal warning for poor performance • Giving someone a performance review that doesn't align with their expectations • Having a conversation with someone about inappropriate clothing • Implementing a restructure that has a bad outcome for the person I am talking to • Managing a friend who is not performing at the level required • Standing up to a dominant member of the team • Talking to someone about allegations of bullying • Telling someone they can't have the leave they have asked for • Terminating someone's employment for poor performance

Managing outside: Dealing with clients, customers, business partners and/or consultants	• Dealing with a consultant who has not been meeting agreed KPIs • Dealing with angry, difficult customers • Managing a business partner who just doesn't get it

As shown by the examples in table 1.1, hard conversations in the workplace cover the spectrum of positional power. They can be when managing up (with the chair, the CEO, the partner, the direct manager, the Minister), across (with peers and other colleagues at similar levels) and down (direct reports and others who are lower in the organisational hierarchy). Hard conversations can also involve external players such as customers, consultants and business partners. The conversation can occur in a one-on-one situation or in a group meeting.

The takeaway is that you will experience daily a broad range of challenging scenarios throughout your working career. The more senior you get, the more important it becomes to deal with these situations early and effectively. It is not just about managing the super-hard conversations that make you dread going to work. There is a continuum in terms of difficulty. If you can get good at having the lower level hard conversations, you enhance your ability to have the really tough ones. Similar to an Olympic diver, if you can master the basic dives first, you can then move on the next level. Before you know it, you are landing dives that win you the gold medal.

The best organisations encourage their people to have the tough conversations, and help them develop their skills to do so. Organisations that don't do this suffer – they don't perform as well because they're not having the robust discussions that contribute to creative ideas and good decisions.

WHAT MAKES HARD CONVERSATIONS HARD?

In my workshops, after we clarify what we mean by hard conversations, I ask people, 'What makes these conversations hard?' I ask this question because often people don't give this a great deal of thought, and understanding what's causing your discomfort is very useful.

Some common responses in my workshops include:

- 'I don't like conflict.'
- 'Hard conversations put the relationship at risk, and I value the relationship.'
- 'The level of emotion makes me feel uncomfortable.'
- 'I don't enjoy upsetting people. I like to be liked. If there's a risk of upsetting someone, I just avoid going there.'
- 'I fear getting an adverse reaction!'
- 'It's frustrating talking to someone who just doesn't want to hear what you have to say. It's not worth the effort.'
- 'It's hard because I have less power and it's very difficult (and risky) having a conversation with someone who is more powerful than I am.'
- 'It takes too long; I don't have the time.'
- 'They're hard because they require a level of skill that I don't have; I just feel completely out of my comfort zone.'
- 'I feel out of control – the uncertainty of the response makes me feel uneasy.'

So, while many things contribute to making a conversation difficult, the core factors seem to be:

1. *The high level of emotion.* Conversations that see us edge into 'fight/flight' make us uncomfortable.

2. *A lack of confidence in conflict situations.* People feel out of their depth. They worry about the uncertainties and emotions that come with the conversation.

3. *The power differential.* Managing up, in particular, brings with it certain risks.

We all must manage what Dan Dana, mediator, psychologist and author of *Managing Differences*, talks about as our 'wrong reflexes'. Our evolutionary flight or fight responses, which cause us to want to either run like crazy or meet force with force to avoid danger, are part of our DNA. While these reflexes were fantastic in helping us escape from or scare away the sabre-tooth tiger and other predators, they are less useful in the modern workplace. But these reflexes still come into play in the workplace. We react to perceived threats in ways that don't really help. As I explore further in chapter 4, a big part of getting better at managing conflict and hard conversations is learning how to regulate our wrong reflexes.

Feeling confident that you can have hard conversations is important. A key aim of this book is to help you feel more confident in having hard conversations by providing you with a model, process and tools to navigate action. I go through these in chapters 3, 4 and 5.

Conversations are more difficult when dealing with people who have more organisational or structural power. The model I outline in this book seeks to recognise the nuances of power in the relationship. I explore how you can factor in the realities of the power dynamic to manage the conversation.

Understanding why you find certain conversations hard helps you deal with the situation. You can develop better strategies and tactics. Of course, understanding what makes a conversation hard often doesn't make it easier to have the conversation. However, my experience is that if you have an awareness of what is making the conversation difficult, you can refine and develop your approach and increase the prospect of getting the outcome you desire.

For example, when you understand you're concerned about having a conversation because you feel what you have to say might damage the relationship, you can explore how you engage with the person in a way that they feel respected and see you as being reasonable. Sometimes that is difficult, such as when you need to tell somebody their performance is not meeting your expectations. But with a little planning and practice, it is possible!

WHY SHOULD YOU BOTHER HAVING HARD CONVERSATIONS?

Why should you bother having conversations that you find uncomfortable? You have four principal reasons to push through the discomfort zone:

1. Organisations expect leaders to have hard conversations.
2. Failing to have hard conversations can cause significant harm to your team and organisation.
3. Failing to have hard conversations can be expensive.
4. Failing to have hard conversations can cause significant damage to individual health and wellbeing.

Organisational expectations of leaders

Leaders are expected to not only have hard conversations, but also do them well. And this is the expectation in the private and public sectors. The New South Wales Government, for example, has developed a set of capabilities – the NSW Public Sector Capability Framework – used to help develop their leaders. Many of the capabilities in this framework allude to the ability to have hard conversations, including the following:

- *Display resilience and courage:* Be open and honest, prepared to express your views, and willing to accept and commit to change.

- *Communicate effectively:* Communicate clearly, actively listen to others, and respond with understanding and respect.

- *Work collaboratively:* Collaborate with others and value their contribution.

- *Influence and negotiate:* Gain consensus and commitment from others, and resolve issues and conflicts.

- *Manage and develop people:* Engage and motivate staff, and develop capability and potential in others.

- *Optimise business outcomes:* Manage people and resources effectively to achieve public value.

- *Manage reform and change:* Support, promote and champion change, and assist others to engage with change.

All these capabilities require leaders to be skilled in having hard conversations. Similar frameworks exist for other government departments and corporate businesses.

Leadership development instruments also seek to assess how well leaders communicate, hold people accountable and manage conflict. For example, the Hogan 360 is a highly regarded 360 feedback instrument developed by Peter Berry Consultancy. It asks peers, managers and reports to rate the leader in relation to:

- communication skills

- influencing and negotiation skills

- holding others accountable for completing their work

- holding people accountable to the organisation's values and expectations

- recognising and challenging poor performance in others.

My experience is that when leaders consistently avoid hard conversations, their colleagues, team members and bosses start suggesting they are not up to the job. Being known as somebody who won't have these hard conversations damages your reputation as a leader.

It's useful to ask yourself, 'What would people think of me as a leader if I fail to have this conversation?' In short, we expect leaders to have hard conversations and manage conflict, so it makes sense to develop your ability to do so.

Possible harm to your organisation

When an issue that needs to be discussed isn't addressed, the problem rarely goes away. Often, things fester and get worse. This can have a terrible impact on your organisation and its people.

During the past 10 years, I have mediated numerous workplace disputes between individuals. The scenarios have included:

- CEOs having problems with members of their executive teams
- partners being unable to work together at various professional service firms
- individuals having difficulty working together in the same team
- managers in conflict with members of their team
- people from separate teams who are clashing.

Almost all these situations could have been resolved without the need for mediation if the individuals had talked through the issues when they first arose. By avoiding the conversation, things got worse. Small misunderstandings became major disputes. This affected not only the individuals at the heart of the dispute, but also people around them. Tension in the workplace made life unpleasant for anyone in the vicinity. Sometimes people who were affected left the organisation or moved to other divisions. Workplace productivity always suffered. When people choose silence, rather than expressing their issues, organisations lose.

The best organisations ensure their leaders have the skills to create psychologically safe environments. They develop leaders who are comfortable having hard conversations. Indeed, the authors of *Crucial Conversations* (Kerry Patterson, Joseph Grenny, Ron McMillan and Al Switzler) highlight that their own research over a 25-year period, and the research of others, clarifies that the key to organisational success comes down to how people handle hard conversations:

> Within high-performing companies, when employees fail to deliver on their promises, colleagues willingly and effectively step in to discuss the problem. In the worst companies, poor performers are first ignored and then transferred. In good companies, bosses eventually deal with problems. In the best companies, everyone holds everyone else accountable – regardless of level or position.

The significant harm that can follow a failure to create a culture of psychological safety is highlighted by Amy Edmondson in *The Fearless Organization*. In the book, Edmondson shares the story of the 2003 Space Shuttle Columbia disaster. She notes that the culture of NASA meant that an engineer who held critical information felt unable to speak up in front of his superiors. Had he done so, the disaster that saw seven astronauts perish when the shuttle re-entered earth's atmosphere most likely would not have occurred. Failing to step up and have the hard conversation has consequences.

Possible expense to your organisation

Organisations where people have the skills and confidence to have hard conversations have less disruptive conflict than their competitors. And this has a real financial benefit.

Dan Dana developed a successful global business providing mediation and conflict-resolution services to corporate, government and not-for-profit businesses. In his early days, Dana had difficulty convincing some of his potential clients to invest in his services. The CFOs asked him to justify the cost of his programs. So what did Dana do? He developed a financial model that allowed CFOs to input data and assess the actual cost of poorly managed conflict in their organisations. As Dana highlights in *Managing Differences*, he was able to show that 'unmanaged employee conflict is perhaps the largest reducible cost in organizations today, and probably the least recognised.'

The Dana Measure of Financial Cost of Organizational Conflict assesses several factors that have a real impact on an organisation's bottom line. The model considers:

- time wasted by managers on unproductive conflict
- the impact of conflict on the quality of decisions
- losing skilled employees and the cost of replacing them
- lower job motivation
- the cost associated with absenteeism.[1]

Studies on the time leaders waste on managing conflict suggest that the percentage is somewhere between 20 and 40 per cent.[2] If an organisation has 100 leaders each being paid an average of $150,000 per year, that amounts to a $15 million loss, excluding on-costs. If only 15 per cent of leader time is spent on conflict that could have been avoided, your organisation is still wasting $2,250,000 on wages each year over 100 leaders. When you add the on-costs associated with these 100 leaders, the actual cost becomes even higher.

When you think about the costs associated with people leaving organisations, the losses become even more tangible. For example, if you need to recruit 10 new leaders each year because of unresolved conflict, and the recruiters charge you 20 per cent of the $150,000 salary, you are up for $300,000. And this does not even factor in the costs associated with lost productivity, interviewing time, and any orientation or training costs.

When I think about the disputes I have worked on involving conflict in professional services firms, the managing partners who engaged me recognised the serious financial risk of losing one or both partners. Often, well-established partners take their clients with them, resulting in a significant reduction in revenue to the firm.

The bottom line is that organisations that help their people develop the skills and confidence to have hard conversations get real financial benefits.

Possible damage to mental health and wellbeing

Not having the hard conversation and allowing conflict to fester takes a toll on you, the other person and anyone else caught up in the conflict. When I'm coaching or mediating people who find themselves in disputes, both parties almost always tell me they are feeling stressed and unhappy with the situation. Often, the ongoing dispute is having an adverse impact on their emotional and physical wellbeing. Research on workplace stress clarifies that poorly managed and unresolved conflict leads to high levels of stress and trauma for everyone involved.[3]

If you can learn how to have effective hard conversations when you need to, you can avoid this unnecessary stress and trauma.

... But there are exceptions

While there are many reasons to have hard conversations, sometimes it makes sense not to go there. If you are dealing with people who are totally unresponsive to what you have to say, the conversation may not be worth having. (I talk about how you might engage with these sorts of individuals in chapter 8). If having the conversation is going to be a career limiting move, holding back makes sense. But, more often than not, when something important is at stake, it makes sense to speak up.

Speaking up requires confidence and skill – and that's what this book is all about. I provide you with a structure, framework and tips to get better at having hard conversations. It won't happen overnight, but with a bit of focus and application, I can promise you will improve your confidence and ability to express your voice. And you will become a better leader.

Recognising the value of having hard conversations is useful. However, knowing you should be doing something and feeling confident enough to do it are two different things. The next chapter begins the process of closing the knowing–doing gap. I start with a bit of self-reflection and ask: how do you currently manage conflict?

Key points

- We all have hard conversations every day. They're the conversations that make us feel uncomfortable, and they can be about everyday stuff or big issues. Often we want to avoid them.

- Hard conversations are hard for a few reasons:
  - They often involve high levels of emotion and can put relationships at risk. We don't want to damage relationships.
  - They often involve conflict. Conflict makes most of us uncomfortable, and we do our best to avoid it. The fear of conflict and the uncertainty that comes with it often drives our decision to avoid a conversation.
  - Hard conversations can involve dealing with people who have more power than we do. This makes the conversation tricky and challenging because we lack the skills and confidence to have them. The lack of confidence means we hold back, often to our detriment.
- You need to push through the discomfort zone for four reasons:
  1. You avoid damaging your reputation as a leader. We expect leaders to have hard conversations. It's part of the gig.
  2. You avoid causing significant harm to your organisation. When you have an issue and you fail to discuss it, the problem rarely goes away. Often, things fester and get worse. Morale and productivity suffer.
  3. By having the conversation and resolving the conflict, you will save the organisation a lot of money.
  4. You avoid the real risk to individual health and wellbeing. Poorly managed conflict leads to high levels of stress for everyone involved.
- In some circumstances it makes sense not to have the hard conversation. Sometimes you need to bide your time. However, when something important is at stake and you feel you should say something, you and the organisation will usually be better off if you do.

- Working through the emotional discomfort that comes with hard conversations can be difficult. These conversations take time and effort. The question you need to ask yourself is this: can you afford not to have the conversation? Time and effort spent today may well save you considerable time and pain in the future.

Action for right now

Think about your own work history. When have you, or the people you work with, failed to have the hard conversations that needed to be had? What were the consequences?

CHAPTER 2

How do you currently manage conflict?

If you want to get better at something, the first thing you need to do is step back and look at what you are doing now. Understanding what you do well and what you do less well is a threshold step if you want to improve. This is certainly the case with hard conversations. To become better at having hard conversations, you need to take the time to reflect on what you currently do, so you can see your strengths and opportunities. This chapter is about becoming more aware of your current behaviour when in conflict. I ask you to consider three questions:

1. How do you currently behave when faced with conflict?

2. What sorts of things trigger you?

3. How do you currently prepare for a hard conversation?

I draw on a useful model of conflict to help you explore what you currently do that's constructive, what do you do that's destructive and what sort of situations might get you into trouble.

SELF-AWARENESS IS IMPORTANT

Being self-aware is important. Socrates suggested that it was necessary to 'know thyself' and that the 'unexamined life is not worth living'. He defined self-knowledge in terms of understanding the limits of one's performance capabilities – that is, knowing your strengths and shortcomings. If you look at elite sport today, every decent coach and player in every sport imaginable spends hours reviewing their most recent performances to identify their strengths, weaknesses and opportunities to improve. Like Socrates, they recognise that understanding your current pattern of behaviour is the first step to improving your performance.

As a leader, you need to think about yourself as a corporate athlete. You perform at your best when you are self-aware. Respected psychologists Rodney Warrenfeltz and Trish Kellett emphasise this in *Coaching the Dark Side of Personality*, noting 'self-awareness forms the baseline from which to evaluate current performance and establish a target for future performance'.

Gaining a better understanding of your current behaviour in conflict

Understanding how people behave during conflict was exactly the focus of Sal Capobianco, Mark Davis and Linda Kraus, three professors from the School of Psychology at Eckerd College in St Petersburg, Florida, back in 1997.

The Leadership Development Institute (LDI) at Eckerd College had been using Thomas-Kilmann conflict 'style' assessment in their Executive Leadership Development Programs. This assessment identifies five major styles of conflict management – collaborating, competing, avoiding, accommodating and compromising. However, the LDI wanted something that was more behaviourally focused. The thinking was that style instruments, while useful, did not allow executives the clarity needed to help them change their behaviour. Having looked around for a behaviourally focused instrument without success, they asked Capobianco, Davis and Kraus to develop one.

Davis and his colleagues believed that 'while conflict itself is inevitable, ineffective and harmful responses to conflict can be avoided, and beneficial responses to conflict can be learned'. They set about developing an instrument that would allow leaders to gain a greater understanding of how they typically respond to conflict so that they would be better equipped and motivated to change their behaviour to improve their performance.

What they came up with is now known as the Conflict Dynamics Profile (CDP), an instrument I have been using with my clients for the past 10 years. The instrument asks a series of questions about how you behave before, during and after conflict. Once you complete these questions, you get a report that shows how you score on 'constructive' and 'destructive' behaviours in conflict, compared to a statistically 'normal' distribution of results.

An overview of a useful model: The Conflict Dynamics Profile

The CDP is not the only instrument around that helps people understand how they manage conflict but it is the best one I've come across, because it focuses on behaviour rather than the fuzzier concept of conflict style.[1]

An instrument that has a pure behavioural orientation is cleaner and more useful when your focus is on gaining information to facilitate change.

In researching and developing the instrument, Capobianco, Davis and Kraus identified a series of behaviours that were common when leaders handled conflict well (constructive behaviours), as well as common behaviours that were displayed when conflict went pear-shaped (destructive behaviours). Within each of these two categories, they identified that some behaviours were more active and others more passive.

Table 2.1 illustrates the various behaviours identified during conflict that are examined in the CDP.

Table 2.1: Behaviours during conflict

	Constructive	**Destructive**
Active	Perspective taking	Winning at all costs
	Creating solutions	Displaying anger
	Expressing emotions	Demeaning others
	Reaching out	Retaliating
Passive	Reflective thinking	Avoiding
	Delaying responding	Yielding
	Adapting	Hiding emotion
		Self-criticising

It is useful to flesh out what each of these behaviours involve.

Active constructive behaviours
The active constructive behaviours usually involve proactive action that reduces tension in a conflict.

Perspective taking
Perspective taking involves stepping into the shoes of the other person and seeing the situation from their perspective. You consciously try to block out how you see the situation and take the time to listen

to the other person and understand what's going on for them. This is an important skill for effective leadership and relationship management, which I explore further in chapter 3.

Creating solutions

Creating solutions during conflict sees you working collaboratively with the other person to address the issues and come up with options to move forward. You're exchanging ideas, sharing concerns frankly and attempting to generate mutually acceptable solutions in a respectful way.

Expressing emotions

Effective communicators often share their feelings during conflict. This isn't to say they unleash all of their emotions; rather, they share the emotions that help the other person understand where they're coming from. For example, they're unlikely to say, 'You make me so angry', because that's not going to add value to the conversation. Instead, they might say something like, 'Look, I'm concerned that if we do it the way you're suggesting, we might upset the client.' Expressing that you are angry is rarely constructive, while expressing that you're concerned can be useful, because the other person may not want you to be concerned or may want to understand why you're concerned. By expressing your emotions in a selective and constructive way, you can help the other person gain a better understanding of where you're coming from and reduce misunderstandings and confusion. You also come across as honest and authentic – both attributes that help build trust and relationships.

Sometimes people challenge the suggestion that expressing emotions is inherently constructive. They argue that it's constructive to manage and withhold your emotions at work. Of course, they're partly correct. My take is that the CDP creators are saying that it's often useful to share emotions during conflict, but not all your emotions. The emotions that are relevant and useful are the ones you want to share. Knowing which emotions to share requires judgement from each of us in different situations. Nevertheless, good leaders do this when they are immersed in conflict.

Reaching out

Reaching out is a behaviour that typically occurs when two parties have had a falling out or reached an impasse. Effective conflict managers recognise the situation and reach out to get things moving and repair the emotional damage caused by the conflict. This may involve making a phone call, walking into the other person's office or some other proactive gesture. It may involve an apology, when appropriate, which can be incredibly powerful in getting two people to rebuild the relationship and begin communicating again. This takes courage and maturity.

Often when things have gone bad, the other party will reject the overture. But if nobody takes the initiative, the conflict will almost inevitably linger and get worse. Reaching out is often the result of someone taking a bigger picture perspective and thinking about what they want to achieve for the organisation, rather than dwelling on any personal discomfort or irritation.

Passive constructive behaviours

In addition to active constructive behaviours, the following passive constructive behaviours are also useful in serving to reduce tension and resolve disputes. However, keep in mind they often have less impact on how people see you as a leader.

Reflective thinking

Reflective thinking relates to taking the time to think things through and analyse the situation before determining how you're going to proceed. In chapter 3, I share a framework to help you get better at having hard conversations. An important part of that framework is self-reflection, which involves aspects of reflective thinking as measured in the CDP, but also goes a whole lot further. Through this framework, I take a deeper look at what's going on for you in the situation.

Delaying responding

Delaying your response during a conflict involves a conscious decision to hold back from responding until the situation settles down. People who do this recognise the heightened emotional state of the other person and realise that, in that moment, responding isn't going to help. Delaying may involve suggesting that you take a short break, adjourning the meeting until later in the day, or diplomatically leaving the situation until things settle down. Note that this behaviour is not about avoiding the situation or the conversation; instead, it involves deliberately delaying participating in the conversation until the other person's more likely to listen to what you have to say. A large part of knowing when to delay your response is picking up on non-verbal cues.

Adapting

Adapting involves being flexible, staying positive and making the best of the situation. Adaptability is also one of the key behaviours used to measure resilience.

Active destructive behaviours

The active destructive behaviours identified in the CDP represent various fight/flight behaviours I mention in chapter 1. The description of these behaviours in the instrument as 'destructive' needs to be put into context. The behaviours are not in themselves destructive. Rather, when they become consistent patterns, they tend to be destructive because they compromise your ability to engage with others and resolve conflict when it arises. Let's drill into the active destructive behaviours.

Winning at all costs

Winning at all costs behaviour involves putting yourself above the team. It's when someone always needs to be right or have the last word. It's when someone refuses to alter their position no matter what. Of course, winning or seeking to win a contest or a pitch is not a bad thing. But when you have someone within the team who always needs to prevail, it can be problematic and quite destructive.

Displaying anger

People display anger in different ways – for example, by raising their voice, shouting, threatening or being physically violent. When someone displays anger in the workplace, people do not forget. It has a lasting effect and often damages relationships. Think about a time someone expressed their anger at you and how it affected you – no doubt it was quite traumatic. While expressing anger can on rare occasions be used tactically, most displays of anger are the result of high levels of emotion and a lack of control. Displaying anger usually inflames a conflict in a non-productive way.

Keep in mind, as discussed earlier, that expressing anger is quite different from constructively expressing your emotions.

Demeaning others

Demeaning others is surprisingly common in the workplace. This behaviour shows up in sarcastic comments, eye rolling or putting down other people's views or ideas. People often try to dress their demeaning comments up as humour, but for those involved, the truth is clear. The behaviour is hurtful and unhelpful.

Retaliating

Retaliating involves trying to get back at the other person for some perceived grievance. It can be a conscious exercise of extracting revenge (a 'dish best served cold'), or a passive attempt to obstruct another person. In any event, this behaviour is highly likely to damage the relationship and exacerbate the conflict.

Passive destructive responses

Passive responses represent the 'flight' behaviours in the fight/flight response, and are common in the workplace.

Avoiding

Avoiding involves keeping away from or ignoring a person who you are having conflict with. As I discuss in chapter 1, it's a common response to conflict and one that can sometimes be helpful, but when it becomes a default pattern it's a problem.

Yielding

Yielding involves giving in to the other person to avoid further conflict and make life easier. At times, yielding makes sense – for instance, when you are disagreeing with the CEO, it will probably help your career to give ground and yield. But if you find yourself constantly giving ground when people challenge your ideas, a pattern of yielding develops – and this is not good for you or the organisation. You will most likely resent having given ground when you really thought you were right, and the organisation misses out if you were.

Hiding emotions

People will often hide their emotions even when they are upset, especially in the work environment. For some people, this is because they don't feel able to express themselves well, while others just don't feel comfortable sharing their emotional state. Why would this be labelled a destructive behaviour? Because hiding emotions creates internal stress and compromises effective communication. The reality is that emotions can't really be hidden – they tend to leak and find expression in non-helpful ways, such as sarcastic comments or over-reactions to small things. And failing to share your emotions often leads people to see you as not caring or lacking authenticity. So, the authors of the CDP suggest that sharing emotions is constructive, while hiding emotions is largely unhelpful.

Labelling this behaviour as destructive sometimes generates discussion in my workshops, and cultural differences need to be acknowledged. Many cultures are uncomfortable sharing their emotions in the same ways as others. Nevertheless, whether you agree with the description or not, it is useful to be conscious of some of the negative consequences of hiding your emotions during conflict.

Self-criticising

Self-criticising is when you go back to your desk and ask yourself things like, 'Why did I say that?' or 'Why didn't I say this?' It's when you replay the incident over and over in your mind (often in the wee hours of the morning), finding fault with how you handled the situation. A fine line exists between seeking to continuously improve and destructive self-criticism. When you sit at your desk criticising yourself, you're not doing any work. When you lie awake at night thinking about the situation, you're disrupting your sleep and damaging your health. Learning from your mistakes can be useful – but overdoing the self-criticism is a destructive behaviour.

Client experience of the CDP

Numerous clients of mine have benefited from a greater awareness of their current behaviour during conflict. A couple of years ago, I was asked to work with Peter and Michael, two partners at a professional services firm. They headed an important group within the firm and had several junior staff working with them, many of whom were expected to work with both partners. They were both experienced and talented professionals, but they had vastly different working styles and personalities. Over time, their relationship went from solid, to poor, to terrible. By the time I was asked to work with them, they had stopped talking to each other. You can imagine the trauma this was causing within the team and the stress that it was creating for them.

The managing partner and the human resources director were at their wits' end. Neither Peter nor Michael was happy with the situation. Both were talking about leaving the firm, which would have been a terrible outcome. Each partner blamed the other and felt they themselves had done little to contribute to the situation. As part of the coaching, Peter and Michael completed the CDP. Of course, these kinds of instruments are only as good as the data that goes into them. I asked both partners to complete the survey honestly, which they did – knowing that no-one else was going to see the results. (I was coaching them separately at this point.)

When we reviewed their reports in the private sessions, they both had high scores on many of the destructive behaviours. As we discussed their results in private, they each acknowledged that they may have contributed to the breakdown in the relationship. This increase in self-awareness allowed us to then proceed with some constructive joint coaching, which resulted in the repair of what was an important working relationship.

How are you behaving in conflict?

To get a sense of how you're currently behaving, in terms of the constructive and destructive behaviours measured by the CDP, complete the following short insight survey.

How do you currently behave in conflict?

Think about your past behaviour in conflict and check the appropriate box.

Constructive behaviours	Never	Sometimes	Often
Perspective taking			
Creating solutions			
Expressing emotions			
Reaching out			
Reflective thinking			
Delaying responding			
Adapting			
Destructive behaviours	**Never**	**Sometimes**	**Often**
Winning at all costs			
Displaying anger			
Demeaning others			
Retaliating			
Avoiding			
Yielding			
Hiding emotion			
Self-criticising			

If you want to get a better understanding of how you're behaving in conflict, a certified CDP practitioner can help you get a clearer picture.[2] It's sometimes difficult to accept you've played a role in creating or contributing to the conflict. If you can step back and accept that almost all conflicts involve contribution by more than one person, you can own your own behaviour and use that awareness to move forward.

WHAT ARE YOUR TRIGGERS WHEN YOU ARE IN CONFLICT?

Another aspect of being self-aware is being conscious of the people, situations and events that trigger you – that is, the things that increase the prospect of you losing your cool during conflict and saying something you might regret. From time to time, we all experience a situation or a person who causes us to overreact. So understanding the sorts of people and situations that tend to trigger you is useful. This can help reduce the prospect of you reacting rather than responding during a conflict. If you can keep your cool and respond rather than react, you will greatly increase the prospect of getting a satisfactory resolution of the situation.

In *Conflict Management Coaching: The CINERGY Model*, Cinnie Noble talks about 'the (not so) merry-go-round of conflict', outlining a process of conflict.[3] Noble suggests that a precipitating interaction occurs in this process, involving incidents where you begin to experience 'discordant thoughts and emotional or other responses about the other person'. At some point in this interaction, you're triggered by specific words or actions that the other person says or does, which creates negative emotions. According to Noble, a trigger can be 'a specific action or word, attitude, tone of voice or facial expression that evokes negative emotion in us'. The trigger will often relate to our values, needs or aspects of our identity 'that we perceive are being challenged, threatened, or undermined by the other person's provoking actions or words'.

This means what triggers you may be completely different from what triggers me. I'm not fussed by people who are five minutes late to meetings, but I've met people who go ballistic in this situation and lock people out of the room. We all respond differently to different situations.

The creators of the CDP identified nine 'hot buttons', which their research suggested were likely to upset people and potentially cause conflict in the workplace. The nine hot button behaviours are being:

1. unreliable

2. overanalytical

3. unappreciative

4. aloof

5. a micromanager

6. self-centred

7. abrasive

8. untrustworthy

9. hostile.

This is clearly not an exhaustive list of triggers. It simply represents nine commonly identified workplace hot buttons. Having used the CDP with over 2000 people over the past 10 years, I know that some people don't get triggered by many of these hot buttons at all. But, interestingly, when we discuss the concept of hot buttons and trigger points, almost all participants resonate with Noble's notion of reacting when their values, needs or sense of identity were being threatened or undermined.

Going back to Peter and Michael, the two partners in the professional service firm I worked with, the idea of being more conscious of their triggers during conflict became particularly important as we worked to rebuild their relationship. They were so different in personality and values that a lot of triggers were coming into play. Once they gained greater insight into what was irritating them, they both became more balanced and less reactive when they were interacting.

A greater tolerance of their differences seemed to develop, along with a willingness to slow down and talk things through.

For example, one of the partners liked to work in the office all the time so he could readily access staff who he wanted to speak with. He reacted to the fact that his partner liked working from home and wasn't readily available. He was also a detail person who wanted to make sure that everybody received crystal clear instructions, while his partner liked to empower people to use their own approaches to resolving problems once briefed. Once they identified these different approaches and understood their motivations and reactions, the relationship changed.

Exploring your triggers

Table 2.2 lists possible values and needs. Which are important to you? Try to come up with your top 10. Then think about whether any of these values have been involved in any of your past conflicts.

Table 2.2: Work values and needs

Accountability	Friendship	Respect
Achievement	Influence	Responsibility
Affiliation	Independence	Results
Altruism	Integrity	Rules
Aesthetics	Hedonism	Security
Analysis	Learning	Self-development
Autonomy	Lifestyle	Stability
Challenge	Loyalty	Structure
Commerce	Order	Teamwork
Compassion	Patience	Trust
Control	Perfection	Tradition
Creativity	Perseverance	Variety
Data	Power	Work–life balance
Excitement/risk	Process	Working conditions
Fairness	Prestige	Work relationships
Fun	Performance	Technical competence
Financial reward	Recognition	

Now using table 2.3, identify some of the behaviours that have caused you to react rather than respond in past conflict situations. Which behaviours caused you to feel disrespected, compromised or threatened? What core value is involved here?

Table 2.3: Possible trigger behaviours

• Assuming I know something that I don't	• Making unfair or false assertions or assumptions
• Being excluded (fear of missing out)	• Micro-managing me
• Being rude or discourteous	• Not listening to what I have to say
• Bullying or intimidating behaviour	• Not respecting my role, position, experience
• Constant whinging/complaining	• Saying I have said something that I didn't say (misrepresenting what I have said)
• Failing to express an opinion	
• Failing to fulfil promises	
• Ignoring my opinion	• Talking about me behind my back
• Implying I have bad intent when I don't	• Talking over me/interrupting me when I'm speaking
• Lying to me	• Yelling or raising voice at me

It can be challenging identifying your own triggers. If you're struggling, talking to somebody who's close to you – such as a mentor, friend or coach – might be worthwhile. Alternatively, you might find it useful to complete the CDP and ascertain your hot buttons. If you want to try to get a better handle on your work values, you could take one of the many free surveys available online – for example, the work values test (available at www.123test.com/work-values-test).

HOW DO YOU CURRENTLY PREPARE FOR HARD CONVERSATIONS?

When you have a tough conversation coming up, what do you do? Do you spend hours strategising about how you're going to deal with it, or do you just take a deep breath and see how it goes? In the next chapter, I introduce you to a valuable approach for preparing for hard conversations. Before considering that approach, however, it's useful to take some time to reflect on how you currently prepare, recognising what you're already doing well and identifying the opportunities for improvement.

Last year, I was running one of my Hard Conversation programs and had a guy called Leon attend. Early in the program, we were talking about how people react to conflict. Many people in the room were sharing their aversion to having hard conversations and how they generally avoided them. Leon spoke up, expressing a different perspective: 'I don't have a problem with hard conversations. Never have. I just don't seem to do them very well.' I asked him what he thought was stopping him from doing them well. He responded, 'I'm not really sure and that's why I'm here!' I asked Leon how he prepared for the hard conversations; he paused and then said, 'What do you mean? I just get on with it and say what needs to be said.'

A couple of other people in the group shared that they would think about an issue and try to gather evidence to support it, or support what they wanted to say. But most people in the room said that they also didn't spend much time preparing for the conversation at all. They didn't have time for that sort of stuff.

The reality is that having hard conversations well is like any complex task: the better the preparation, the better the outcome. It's no surprise to me that one of the most common pieces of feedback I get from people after they've completed one of my courses is how valuable they found the preparation process. (I discuss this in detail in chapter 3.) Most people just don't take the time to prepare properly for hard conversations.

Some people say they don't have time to prepare for every hard conversation that comes along. My response to this is, 'Okay, but if you decide you need to have a hard conversation, can you afford not to take the time to prepare properly?' Preparing properly does not necessarily take a lot of time. Once you become familiar with the process I share with you, you can prepare quite quickly. Failing to spend the time preparing for a hard conversation is a high-risk strategy that often ends badly.

Take a moment to think about how you currently prepare for hard conversations using the following checklist.

Preparing for a hard conversation checklist

When you decide to have a hard conversation, do you:	Yes/No
1. Spend time reflecting on the situation?	
2. Talk to others about the best way to handle the conversation?	
3. Gather the information, examples and data you need to help the other person understand what you are planning to say?	
4. Clarify in writing why the issue is important to the organisation or the team?	
5. Think about the situation from the other person's perspective?	
6. Come up with questions that you want to explore with the other person to deepen your understanding of how they see the situation?	
7. Anticipate the objections or questions the other person might have?	
8. Think about how you'll respond to anticipated objections or questions?	
9. Think about how you'll start the conversation?	
10. Have a clear goal and messages for the conversation?	
11. Practise having the conversation with a friend or colleague?	

Remember – most people will struggle to prepare for hard conversations because they don't have a framework to use. The process and framework set out in the next chapter makes preparing for a hard conversation easy.

Key points

- Behavioural self-awareness is the starting point in any leadership development effort. To become better at having hard conversations, you need to reflect on what you currently do so you can see your strengths and identify opportunities to grow.

- The Conflict Dynamics Profile (CDP) provides a useful framework for identifying your constructive and destructive behaviours in conflict. By gaining an understanding of your patterns of behaviour when faced with conflict, you become better equipped to modify your behaviour and increase your effectiveness as a leader.

- Constructive behaviours include perspective taking, creating solutions, expressing emotions, reaching out, reflective thinking, delaying responding and adapting. Destructive behaviours include winning at all costs, displaying anger, demeaning others, retaliating, avoiding, yielding, hiding emotion and self-criticising.

- Understanding the sorts of people and situations that tend to trigger you into a fight/flight type response is useful. This can help reduce the prospect of you reacting, rather than responding, during a conflict. If you can keep your cool and respond rather than react, you will greatly increase the prospect of getting a satisfactory resolution of the situation.

- While we all have different triggers, they often relate to our values, needs or aspects of our identity that we feel are being challenged, threatened or undermined by the other person. The CDP identifies nine common workplace triggers: being unreliable, overanalytical, unappreciative, aloof, a micromanager, self-centred, abrasive, untrustworthy or hostile. While these are common triggers, many other circumstances may cause you to react. The challenge is to identify what these are.

- Reflecting on what you currently do can reveal opportunities for improvement. Having a structured process to help you prepare for hard conversations can save time, reduce stress and contribute to better outcomes.

Action for right now

Think about the way you currently manage conflict. What do you do well? What can you do better?

Think about a recent conflict at work that triggered you. Which of your values or what aspect of your identity was coming into play?

Take the time to think about how you currently prepare for hard conversations. Did you tick off many items on the provided checklist? Or do you tend to 'wing it'?

CHAPTER 3

––––––

Hard conversations made easy: A practical process and framework

In chapter 1, I talk about how challenging hard conversations can be. The risk to relationships and heightened emotion make them tough. In this chapter, I outline a process and framework to improve the way you prepare. This practical approach will help you get the best potential outcome.

A BIT OF BACKGROUND

Frameworks and processes help us grapple with complexity and solve problems. I have taught the process and framework in this book to over 2000 people who have taken my Mastering Hard Conversations program or worked with me as an executive coach over the past 13 years. It's evolved over time and has been influenced by several talented academics and practitioners.[1]

The power of having a useful process and framework for hard conversations was illustrated for me when I worked with Julie. Julie was being reviewed for promotion within her accounting firm. The firm had a rigorous assessment program that involved putting candidates through a series of tests to assess leadership capability. One assessment involved a role-play with an actor who was playing the role of a poorly performing member of Julie's team. The firm had put Julie up for promotion the previous year and she'd bombed out on this hard conversation role-play. After coaching Julie through the framework and practising a few different scenarios, I waited to hear how she performed in her assessment.

She blitzed it. When I asked her what was different between this year and the last, she responded, 'The process. Having a process and framework just made things easier when I was under pressure.'

An outline of the process

My process has six steps:

1. *Self-reflection:* What's going on for you in the conflict?
2. *Perspective taking:* How is the other person seeing the situation?
3. *Open questions:* What would you like to understand?
4. *Common ground:* What do you have in common?
5. *Anticipating objections:* What tough questions and objections do you need to be prepared for?
6. *Clarifying goals and messages:* What are your key goals and messages?

Figure 3.1 shows these six steps, and I walk through each step in more detail in this chapter.

Figure 3.1: The six-step process for hard conversations

STEP 1: SELF-REFLECTION – WHAT'S GOING ON FOR YOU?

To succeed in a hard conversation, it's important at the outset to understand what's going on for you. By having a deep understanding of your own actions, thoughts, feelings and motivations, you increase your ability to stay calm. This will enable you to articulate your key points more clearly. As a result, you will increase the chances of influencing the other person and getting the outcome you'd like.

Sherod Miller is an American social psychologist who has spent a large part of his life helping people to communicate more effectively. He has developed a framework that makes it easier to understand what's going on when you find yourself in conflict.

Miller suggests five things influence your awareness and experience of conflict: sensory data, thoughts, emotions, wants and actions.[2] According to Miller while these components are interrelated, if you focus on them one at a time, you gain a deeper understanding of the situation. An illustration of this framework is set out in figure 3.2.

Figure 3.2: The Circle of Self Reflection

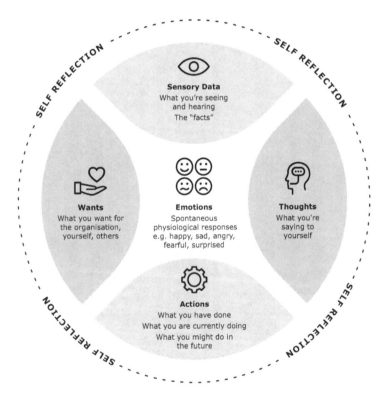

Let's take a moment to consider each of the elements:

- *Sensory data:* Sensory data is your sensory information – the things you see and observe. It's what you read, what you're told, what you hear, and what you touch, smell and taste.

- *Thoughts:* Thoughts are how you're thinking about the issue and the meaning you make of your sensory data. You and I can observe the same sensory data but have very different interpretations. This is because things beyond sensory data shape our thoughts. Our values, sense of identity, assumptions, experiences, biases and expectations all influence our interpretation of the data.

- *Emotions:* Emotions are your feelings about the issue – your spontaneous physiological responses to your experiences. Sensory data and thoughts create emotions. Emotions drive your behaviour, whether or not you are conscious of it. Universal emotions include happiness, sadness, anger, fear, disgust and surprise. But many others are possible. In a conflict, you experience a range of emotions. Often, intense emotions such as anger mask deeper underlying emotions such as fear, disappointment or sadness.

- *Wants:* Wants are your motivations. Bringing a broader 'systems perspective' when thinking about what you want is often useful. Conflict affects the system, not just you and the other person. It's useful to consider:
  - What do you want for your business or organisation?
  - What do you want for the team?
  - What do you want personally?
  - What do you want from the other person?
  - What do you want for the other person?
  - What do you want for clients or customers?
  - What do you want for any other stakeholders?

- *Actions:* Actions can be historical, current, or future. When thinking about your actions, think about what you've done or failed to do that might have contributed to this situation. Also consider what you are doing and might potentially do. For example, one of my current clients, Jessica, admitted that on several occasions she had failed to share her concerns with one of her team members. This had contributed to the current awkward situation where she had to explain that the team member's performance wasn't satisfactory. Jessica realised that if she'd shared her concerns earlier, the current hard conversation would probably not have been necessary.

When self-reflecting about a situation, ask yourself five questions:

1. What is my sensory data?
2. What am I thinking?
3. How am I feeling?
4. What do I want?
5. What have I done (or not done), that's contributed to the situation?

An illustration of self-reflecting

To illustrate how you self-reflect, I'm going to share a scenario experienced by one of my clients. Helen was having difficulties working with her new boss, Adrian. They had different work styles, and there was some lack of clarity around their respective roles. They regularly clashed at team meetings. Helen was unhappy with the situation, and she realised she needed to talk it through with Adrian before things went from bad to worse.

I asked Helen to think about what was going on for her, focusing on the five areas in The Circle of Self Reflection shown in figure 3.2. In figure 3.3, I summarise what she had to say about her perception of her conflict with Adrian (her boss).

Figure 3.3: Self-reflecting about a conflict – Helen

Actions
- I've been a bit sharp with Adrian
- I've challenged Adrian in front of others
- I have tended to withdraw rather than discuss things
- I've forcefully supported my team

SELF-REFLECTION
(Helen reflecting on what's going on for her)

Sensory Data
- Adrian saying "do it my way"
- Adrian getting upset when I express a contrary view
- Adrian raising his voice and closing me down
- Team members complaining about unreasonable expectations

Wants
- Deliver organisational goals
- Have clarity about my role
- Have a happy, high performing team
- Be respected by Adrian and his boss (be heard)
- Improve my relationship with Adrian (build trust and understanding)

Emotions
- Confused, frustrated, stressed, vulnerable, concerned

Thoughts
- Adrian likes to be in control – he doesn't like to be challenged
- Adrian doesn't like me – I threaten him
- He's aloof and disrespectful
- This can't continue as is – I need to talk to him

Self-reflection during unplanned hard conversations

Many hard conversations happen without warning. Often you don't have time to prepare and use a model such as the one being explained here. When someone charges up to your desk while yelling at you, you don't have time to stay, 'Hang on, I just need a moment to use this framework to work out what's going on for me here.'

However, once you start using this model, and become familiar with it, you will find yourself drawing on it even when you're ambushed. It will become your way of working on conflict. Part of the challenge is, of course, keeping your cool under pressure. I talk about how you can become better at that in chapter 4.

Practising self-reflection

Try using these five areas for self-reflection when working through a past or current situation. What was/is going on for you in this situation? You can also refer to the detailed case studies in chapter 5 to gain a greater understanding of how to use the model.

STEP 2: PERSPECTIVE TAKING – HOW IS THE OTHER PERSON SEEING THE SITUATION?

The second step in my process is to understand the other person's perspective. Comprehending how someone sees a situation the way they do is sometimes difficult. At first, you might think they are being totally unreasonable. You need to slow down and step into the shoes of the other person. They think they are being reasonable. The aim is to understand how they see the situation.

If you become skilled at seeing the other person's perspective, you change your approach to how you have the conversation. You appreciate alternative possibilities. You temper your initial critical thoughts and become more willing to explore issues and concerns. You will become better at communicating, negotiating and influencing outcomes.

How do you do this?

Let's go back to Adrian and Helen. One of Helen's challenges when preparing to discuss the conflict with Adrian is to understand how Adrian sees the situation.

In our coaching session, I asked Helen to pretend she was Adrian and think how he might complete the Circle of Self Reflection. Figure 3.4 summarises what she came up with trying to see the situation from Adrian's perspective.

Figure 3.4: Perspective taking about a conflict – Adrian

Actions
- Been directive to Helen.
- Dismissed Helen's suggestions a little quickly.

PERSPECTIVE TAKING

(Helen reflecting on Adrian's perspective)

Sensory Data
- My boss saying "you need to fix this!"
- Colleagues telling me how to manage Helen
- Helen interrupting me in meetings
- Helen's staff complaining/ missing deadlines

Wants
- Achieve organisational goals.
- Keep my boss happy.
- A productive, happy team.
- To be treated with respect by Helen.
- Helen and her team to feel respected.
- Develop a better relationship with Helen.

Emotions
- Uncomfortable, surprised, embarrassed, hurt, angry, stressed.

Thoughts
- Helen doesn't respect me. She's rude.
- Helen doesn't like being held accountable.
- Helen needs to manage her team better.
- I need to become a better leader.

Practising perspective taking

Think about the past or current conflict you used when you were practising self-reflection (earlier in this chapter). Now put yourself in the other person's shoes.

You might think that you can never really understand someone else's perspective. And you'd be right. Getting into the head of another person is challenging. It's easier if you know them – but, even then, it can be tricky. Often, you won't know what the other person is thinking, feeling or wanting.

You'll be guessing. Yet, thinking about their perspective can be ground-breaking. You recognise things may not be as simple as you first thought. Their irrational behaviour may not be so irrational after all.

This process helps you identify what you don't know or understand. You can start thinking about some of the questions you'd like to explore in the conversation – which takes us to Step 3.

STEP 3: OPEN QUESTIONS – WHAT WOULD YOU LIKE TO UNDERSTAND?

The third step in the preparation process is about being curious and crafting questions. You want to craft questions that will help you understand the other person's perspective. Generally speaking, you want to ask 'open' rather than 'closed' questions. Open questions invite expansive answers. They often begin with who, what, when or how. Closed questions invite a yes/no response.

To illustrate, in table 3.1 I set out some closed versus open questions.

Table 3.1: Closed versus open questions

Closed question	Open question
Are you angry?	How are you feeling?
Would you like to go to the park?	Where would you like to go?
Do you like my idea?	What do you think of my idea?
Can we start now?	When would you like to start?

Open questions can be incredibly powerful. They can change the way people see you. A great open question signals that you are keen to understand what the other person has to say. Often, they change the tone of the conversation. Conversations that otherwise might become adversarial become civilised dialogue.

Learning to ask open rather than closed questions takes real skill. I explore this fully in chapter 4.

An illustration of open questions

Returning to the Helen and Adrian scenario, I asked Helen to come up with at least five open questions she might like to explore with Adrian at their planned meeting. She came up with the following:

- What do you see as our greatest challenges over the next six to 12 months?

- What are you pleased with?

- What am I doing that is causing you concern?

- How are you finding the way we're working together?

- What are your thoughts on how my team is going?

- If you'd like me to do one thing differently, what would it be?

- What are your boss's expectations over the next 12 months?

- How can I help you manage those expectations?

- How would you feel if I shared some thoughts on how we could improve the way we work together?

A watch point: 'Why'?

You need to be careful when starting questions with 'Why'. While starting a question with why will create an open question, why is risky. When you start a question with why, people will often feel you are judging or criticising them. Better options exist, as shown in table 3.2.

Table 3.2: Finding better options to asking why

Why?	A better alternative
Why did you do that?	When you decided to do *x*, what influenced your decision?
Why didn't you follow procedure?	What caused you to adopt a different approach to the standard procedure?
Why should I accept your recommendation?	How did you determine that this recommendation makes the most sense?

I explore this further in chapter 4.

Practising your why questions

Redraft the following why questions to something that is more likely to generate a constructive response. You might want to refer to Helen's list of open questions for ideas.

Why on earth did you choose this approach?	
Why didn't you call me first?	
Why didn't you do what I suggested?	

STEP 4: COMMON GROUND – WHAT DO YOU HAVE IN COMMON?

When you are involved in a conflict, identifying the common ground is often hard. You and the other person may both want great outcomes for the organisation. You may both respect each other's talents. But this gets lost in the traffic. It can be useful gaining insight into what you both want. If you can identify the common ground, you can generally have a constructive conversation.

Many years ago, I worked with the late David Newton, a pioneer of mediation in Australia. During my training, David emphasised the importance of the mediator identifying common ground and interest between the parties.

'Common ground,' he said, 'is not just agreement about facts or legal issues. It is an expression covering all of the things that the parties can feel positive about, or value each other for.' It covers aspects such as valuing the relationship, wanting a productive and happy workplace, and appreciating each other's expertise.

The common ground is where you find the possibility of resolving the conflict. Focusing on common ground is no less important when you are 'self-mediating' and having hard conversations than it is in formal mediations. In both instances, it provides the seeds for constructive conversation.

Returning to the Helen and Adrian scenario, plenty of common ground can be found:

- They both want the relationship to improve.
- They both want to deliver the desired organisational outcome.
- They both want to be treated with respect and be heard.

Ultimately, this common ground enabled them to rebuild their relationship and improve the way they worked together.

Sometimes, in a hard conversation, there may seem to be simply no common ground. What do you do then? Keep looking – there is almost always something both parties want. For example, if you are making someone redundant, the common ground might be that you both want them to be treated respectfully.

Identifying what the common ground might be is always useful. When you are struggling, you might formulate some open questions to use when you meet. For example, you might say, 'I was wondering what was important for you in this situation' or 'What are the one or two things you really want?' You might follow that up with, 'What don't you want?'

Practising finding common ground

Using the past or current personal scenario you've been working with in previous sections, identify the common ground. What are the two or three things you both want?

STEP 5: ANTICIPATE OBJECTIONS – WHAT TOUGH QUESTIONS DO YOU NEED TO PREPARE FOR?

Sometimes you find yourself blindsided during a hard conversation. A question or objection completely throws you off balance. Suddenly, what seemed clear becomes muddy. To prepare well, you need to anticipate the potential objections and tough questions.

Most people don't bother to do this. If you fail to think about likely objections and questions, however, you increase the chances of being caught off-guard in the conversation. By working through the possible objections, your confidence going into the conversation will skyrocket.

Returning to the Helen and Adrian scenario, Helen identified that Adrian might raise the following objections in the conversation:

- 'I've found you to be quite rude from the time I started in the role.'

- 'You constantly challenge my decisions in front of the staff. It's disrespectful.'

- 'You need to accept that I'm your manager, and sometimes you just have to do what I request, even if you disagree with me.'

- 'You have no idea how much pressure I'm under to make sure we complete this project on time.'
- 'You have not been holding your team accountable, and this is the reason we've fallen behind.'

Having anticipated these objections, Helen can think through what she might say. She can plan to respond in a way that helps resolve the issues, rather than creating more tension. She needs to stay calm, own her behaviour, and bring a curious mindset to the situation. She needs to listen to understand and not to take things personally. Of course, this is easy to say!

Table 3.3 outlines some examples of how Helen might respond to her expected objections.

I spend more time in chapter 4 fleshing out the rationale behind these suggested responses to objections. What's worth noting here is:

- the need to show you have heard the objection
- the value of using open questions to gain a greater understanding of the comment.

You might think you can never anticipate everything someone will say. And that's true. But it's amazing how much you can predict by using the self-reflection and perspective-taking process. You will anticipate most objections and tough questions. By doing the hard work, you create the luxury of being able to plan how to respond before the conversation takes place. This builds confidence.

Anticipating objections is difficult when you don't know the other person well. A useful approach is to ask, 'What would I do if I was in their position?'

Table 3.3: Possible responses to expected objections

Objection	Possible response
'I've found you to be quite rude from the time I started in the role.'	I'm sorry that's how I've come across. It's never my intention to be rude, and it's disappointing to hear that's how you feel. What have I been doing that you have found rude?
'You constantly challenge my decisions in front of the staff. It's disrespectful.'	Yes, I have challenged your decisions in front of the team; that's the way I work. I always believe we should have open, respectful discussions about issues. But I'm concerned that you feel my behaviour is disrespectful. I always try to be respectful, and if I'm not doing that I need to take your feedback on board. What did I do or say that was disrespectful?
'You need to accept that I'm your manager, and sometimes you just have to do what I request, even if you disagree with me.'	I understand that. I guess I would just appreciate being able to talk to you about issues that affect me. I accept that there will be times I will have to accept your decisions when we disagree, but it would be great if you can at least give me a chance to share my views on issues that have a big impact on my role.
'You have no idea how much pressure I'm under to make sure we complete this project on time.'	I'm sorry to hear you are under so much pressure. I want to work with you to ensure we complete the project on time.
'You have not been holding your team accountable, and this is the reason we've fallen behind.'	I've been trying to hold the team accountable. What have you seen that concerns you?

Practising anticipating objections

Think about the personal past or current scenario you've been working on in previous sections and make a list of potential objections or tough questions the other person might ask you.

STEP 6: CLARIFYING – WHAT ARE YOUR KEY GOALS AND MESSAGES?

The last step in this framework is clarifying your goals and key messages for the conversation.

As you head into a hard conversation, you may feel apprehensive. This is a very human response. One thing that will help calm you down is having a couple of clear goals and key messages.

When you have completed the self-reflection and perspective-taking exercises discussed in this chapter, you will be able to identify your key goals and the key messages. Having this clarity increases the likelihood that the conversation will go well. You understand your goals, and you know what you want to say. In contrast, if you go into a conversation without clear goals and messages, your apprehension will be justified.

Start by asking yourself, 'What's my goal/s in this conversation'?

Returning to the Helen and Adrian scenario, Helen's goals might look like this:

- To understand Adrian's perspective about my team and our working relationship.

- To share my concerns and thoughts on how we might improve our working relationship.

- To agree on some specific action to take things forward.

Drawing on the self-reflection and perspective-taking exercises, Helen might list her key messages as follows:

- I want the team to deliver the project on time and want to support Adrian in any way I can.
- I value Adrian's experience and input.
- I want to work collaboratively with Adrian to deliver the best outcomes for the organisation.
- I want to improve our working relationship.
- I appreciate I can sometimes come across as being a bit bullish in meetings and will work to temper that.
- I would like Adrian to listen to my ideas before closing me down.
- I just want to be given a chance to contribute and be heard.
- I know at times I will need to accept Adrian's decision and direction.

Practising finding goals and key messages

- Using the personal past or current scenario you have been working on during this chapter, ask yourself:
  - 'What are my key goals in this situation?'
  - 'What are the key messages I want to ensure that the other person understands?'

You might think that you can't plan for a hard conversation, and that this approach won't work. Consistent feedback from my clients tells me it does. I'm not suggesting you create a script. You need to be in the moment. But, having a few clear goals and key messages allows you to stay on track. When you get taken down a rabbit hole, you'll be able to find your way back to the path.

This chapter focuses on preparing for a hard conversation. In the next chapter, I examine some of the specific skills you need to refine and develop to become more effective during the conversation. In chapter 5, I look at a couple of case studies to illustrate how you can use the framework and process.

Key points

- You can set yourself up to manage just about any tough conversation by asking six key questions:
  1. What's going on for me in this conflict?
  2. What's going on for the other person?
  3. What would I really like to understand?
  4. What's the common ground?
  5. What tough questions and objections do I need to be prepared for?
  6. What are my key goals and messages for this conversation?

- When considering what's going on for you (self-reflecting) and what's going on for the other person (perspective taking), it is useful to consider:
  1. sensory data (what you see and hear)
  2. thoughts (the stories you tell yourself, often shaped by data, values, assumptions and expectations)
  3. emotions
  4. motivations (wants and needs)
  5. actions (both past and present).

- An important part of preparation is coming up with great open questions to help you understand the other person's perspective. Asking open questions can be incredibly powerful, and can signal that you want to understand. They can change the dynamic of a conversation for the better.

- When you're trying to resolve conflict, you will increase the chances of finding an amicable way forward if you identify the common ground.

- By anticipating objections and tough questions, and thinking about how you will address them, you will increase your effectiveness and confidence in the conversation.

- Having clarity around your key goals and key messages for each hard conversation increases the likelihood that the conversation will go well. You know your goals, and you know what you want to say.

- Sometimes my clients say they don't have the time to follow this process. Or they'll say that it's too complicated. Learning anything new is uncomfortable for a short period. But once you get the hang of it, you'll find this process easy. And, as a leader, you'll have plenty of opportunity to practise. Every day, whether they're small or large conflicts, they're going to be there, waiting for you.

Action for right now

Use the framework outlined in this chapter to help prepare for new conflict scenarios. Also think about past scenarios, and use the framework to reflect on what happened and what you could have done better.

CHAPTER 4

Polishing your skills for hard conversations

This chapter focuses on some of the core skills that you need to develop and practise to be more effective during hard conversations. If skill development is the secret to success (and it is), a core question is: how do you become highly skilled?

When I think of Don Bradman, Australian cricketer (and the greatest batsman in the history of test cricket), I recall black and white television footage of a young Bradman honing his batting skills. He used a cricket stump and a golf ball against a large corrugated iron tank at the side of his family home. For those not familiar with cricket, a stump is around 71 centimetres tall and fewer than 4 centimetres in diameter. And the angles of the tank could ping the small golf ball off in unpredictable directions. Bradman spent thousands of hours refining his skills, using this unorthodox and challenging method.

In *Outliers*, Malcolm Gladwell refers to the research of psychologist K. Anders Ericsson in developing complex task expertise, and the work of neurologist Daniel Levitin, who examined Ericsson's and other studies on that same subject.

Levitin noted:

> The emerging picture from the studies is that 10,000 hours of practise is required to achieve the level of mastery associated with being a world-class expert – in anything. In study after study, of composers, basketball players, fiction writers, ice skaters, concert pianists, chess players, master criminals and what have you, this number comes up again and again.

Gladwell shares stories and facts that illustrate how brilliant musicians as diverse as Mozart and the Beatles each demonstrate the 10,000-hour rule. Mozart, who started writing music at six, did not produce his greatest works until he had been composing for over 20 years. The Beatles, prior to their first enormous success in 1964, had performed about 1200 times in Hamburg between 1960 and late 1962 – with multiple performances each night, and usually playing for a total of eight hours a night. John Lennon, talking about the Hamburg experience, noted, 'We got better and got more confidence. We couldn't help it with all the experience playing all night long.'

If you want to become good at hard conversations, you need to develop your skills.

CORE SKILLS FOR HARD CONVERSATIONS

In their course 'Becoming Conflict Competent', Sherod Miller, Craig Runde and Tim Flanagan suggest you need to practise six core skills to become good at hard conversations:

1. staying calm
2. self-reflecting

3. perspective taking

4. listening under pressure

5. asking open questions

6. speaking with clarity.

I examine the skills of self-reflection and perspective taking in chapter 3, so in this chapter I focus on the other four skills.

STAYING CALM

In chapter 1, I talk about the challenge of dealing with the heightened levels of emotion in hard conversations. Managing your fight/flight reactions can be tough, but with practice it can be done. By learning how to stay calm under pressure, you get better at responding, rather than reacting.

What do I mean by responding rather than reacting? When you respond, you have a level of control. The difference may be the few seconds it takes to breathe deeply, but you have a level of composure when you respond that you don't have when you react. Reactions are fight/flight reflexes that can be helpful when our lives are at risk. But in the workplace, you are usually better off responding than reacting.

Let me share a story to illustrate the importance of staying calm. On 14 April 1996, Australian golfer Greg Norman entered the final round of the US Masters at Augusta with a six-shot lead over his great rival Nick Faldo. Norman, a two-time British open winner, had won over 80 tournaments around the world and spent 331 weeks as the world's number one golfer. But he had never won the Masters. He finished runner-up twice – to Jack Nicklaus in 1986, and to Larry Mize in 1987, when Mize miraculously chipped in from a bunker

40 metres from the hole to win the sudden-death playoff. There was no tournament Norman wanted to win more than the Masters.

As a young sports fan, getting up at 4 am to watch Norman lose tragically had become a painful part of my existence, but nothing had prepared me for the traumatic events on 14 April 1996. It was agonising and unforgettable. After leading the tournament for three rounds, Norman cracked under pressure. His emotions got the better of him. He turned a six-stroke lead into a five-stroke loss.

Years of developing all his other golfing skills came to nought because Norman failed to master the ability to stay calm when it counted.

Of course, it's easy to say 'stay calm' and hard to do. At times your fight/flight reflexes will kick in – like they did for Norman – completely screwing things up. But you can reduce the number of times this happens. It's now standard practice for young elite athletes in all sports to develop not only the physical skills needed for their sport, but also the ability to stay calm under pressure. As a leader, you need to learn and practise staying calm under pressure to increase the chances of performing at your best during a hard conversation.

An approach to staying calm

How do you stay calm? When the pressure is on, the best athletes and the best leaders keep their cool. They manage their emotional state without going into fight/flight-mode. How do they do this? For a few rare individuals, being cool and collected under pressure comes naturally. But most Olympic athletes, and the rest of us mere mortals, need to learn over time how to self-regulate and compete at their best.

You can do eight things to help you stay calm during hard conversations.

Prepare

As discussed in chapter 3, having the chance to prepare properly for a hard conversation can help you feel more confident and balanced going into the conversation. I also provide more detail on how you do this in chapter 5.

Practise breathing control techniques

When I ask participants in my Mastering Hard Conversations program, 'What do you do to stay calm in a tough conversation?' the number one answer is always, 'Breathe'. When you observe Olympic athletes immediately before a race or before any high-pressure moment, they almost always seem to focus on their breathing. They slow down, centre, breathe slowly and then proceed with the task. This is something they train to do. It is the single most useful thing you can do if you want to become better at managing your emotions during a challenging conversation.

If you can learn to centre and breathe when under pressure, you can maintain balance during the conversation. Many breathing techniques are available for you to practise. See the sidebar 'Practising controlled breathing' for one option.

Practise mindfulness

Ten years ago I did a course based on the research of Jon Kabat-Zinn, one of the pioneers of mindfulness. In an interview on mindful.org, Kabat-Zinn defines mindfulness as 'paying attention on purpose, in the present moment, and non-judgementally to the unfolding of experience moment by moment'. After my initial attempts at mindfulness, I was pleasantly surprised by the results. Regular practice improved my ability to stay calm under pressure. It's now something that I encourage all my clients to do.

Recent research suggests that regular mindfulness practice improves sleep, concentration and performance. In addition, it has been shown to reduce stress, anxiety and depression.[1]

An easy way to develop your mindfulness skills is to use an app, and many are available. Some are free or have free trials. The apps I recommend to clients are Headspace, Smiling Mind and Calm, but many others are on the market and worth exploring.

Be conscious of your triggers

As discussed in chapter 3, being conscious of your triggers is also useful. Your triggers are the things and people who take you out of your comfort zone and cause your shift from your more responsive prefrontal cortex to the more reptilian reactive parts of your brain. You can learn from your past reactions and change your future behaviour to get better outcomes. Through being aware of your triggers, and knowing how to respond when they appear, you increase your chances of staying calm and responding rather than reacting.

Be curious

When someone is challenging or criticising you, try not to get defensive. Ask open questions to understand where they are coming from. Instead of getting defensive, go exploring!

Be conscious of your physical reactions

Being aware of how you physically react when you're in a heightened emotional state can help you learn how to short-circuit your fight/flight reactions. For example, some people will feel their heart race, others will feel tension in their shoulders and chest, while others will feel sick in the stomach and just want to leave.

If you can become conscious of your physical reactions, you can then bring a cognitive response into the equation. You can mentally disrupt your fight/flight response by saying to yourself, 'Oh, I'm going into fight/flight'. You can then take action to stay calm (taking a slow breath is always a good start).

Name the emotion

Research shows that naming the emotion you're experiencing reduces its intensity.[2] This, in turn, helps you stay calm. For example, if you are conscious of how you physically react when you get angry, say to yourself, 'Oh, I'm getting angry', and then take a breather to calm down and manage your behaviour.

Breathe in the moment

When engaged in a hard conversation, regularly focusing on breathing slowly to stay calm is critical. Again, the following sidebar provides some tips.

Practising controlled breathing

Here's an exercise for practising breathing:

1. Sit on a chair and get comfortable by having your feet flat on the floor and your hands on your lap.

2. With your eyes open, take two slow, deep breaths, breathing in through your nose and out through your mouth.

3. Close your eyes and take four more deep breaths, saying to yourself, 'Relax' as you breathe out.

4. Breathe normally again, being conscious of the movement of your breath. For the next 15 seconds, notice where your body moves as you breathe – feel your chest move, and be aware of any movement in your stomach and diaphragm. Just be conscious of the movement.

5. Take five more breaths, counting silently as you breathe in and out. Count 'one' as you breathe in, and 'two' as you breathe out, continuing until you reach ten.

6. Breathing normally, take 15 seconds to listen to any sounds present, concentrating on what you can hear.

7. Take one last slow deep breath in, exhale, and open your eyes. Notice how you feel.

By practising this sort of breathing technique regularly, you will develop the ability to centre and breathe quickly when under pressure and be able to stay calm when you need to.

Not everyone has the time or inclination to set aside part of their day to practise mindfulness and breathing techniques regularly. If you fit into that category, don't despair. You no doubt already have many opportunities to practise these techniques daily. Every time you drive your car, you most likely experience some bad driving from another driver. They cut you off, fail to give way, come into your lane or are slow to take off when the lights turn green. You will likely feel frustrated. Taking public transport or even riding your bike can cause similar feelings of frustration to arise. In the past, you may have occasionally gotten annoyed. In these situations, if you can consciously practise centring and breathing, it's very useful. Instead of getting annoyed, breathe in and say to yourself, 'Relax' and breathe out.

Another opportunity that comes up is when you receive phone calls. Every day you likely receive numerous calls. At some point, these calls will begin to add to your stress levels. Instead of picking up the phone quickly when you get a call, take a slow breath before you answer, relax as you breathe out, and then pick up the phone. You'll notice the difference. You will feel more composed. These two easy-to-practise exercises will help you develop neural pathways so that when you find yourself under pressure, you'll quickly be able to centre, breathe and stay calm.

LISTENING UNDER PRESSURE

Years ago, I had a sobering listening experience with my older daughter, Claudia. Being a professional coach, I like to think of myself as an excellent listener – someone who enables my clients to feel heard and understood. But during our conversation, Claudia gave it to me straight: 'Dad, you're looking at me, but I can tell you're not listening.' She was right. I wasn't 'really' listening.

Most people recognise that listening is important and will tell you they're good listeners, but the research suggests otherwise. Often, we listen to hear what we want to hear, we listen with a view to shape what we're about to say, or we don't listen at all, even though we're good at making it look as if we're listening.

As Stephen Covey stated in *The 7 Habits of Highly Effective People*:

> Most people do not listen with the intent to understand; they listen with the intent to reply. They're either speaking or preparing to speak. They're filtering everything through their own paradigms, reading the autobiography into other people's lives.

Covey emphasises the importance of empathic listening – that is, listening for feeling and meaning. He suggests that when we listen with a genuine intent to understand, the conversational paradigm changes. When people realise that you have heard and understood what they have to say, they become willing to listen to you. In *Difficult Conversations*, Douglas Stone, Bruce Patton and Sheila Heen make a similar point, noting, 'Listening well is one of the most powerful skills you can bring to a difficult conversation. It helps you understand the other person. And, importantly, it helps them understand you.'

How we listen is a consequence of the way our brains work. The scientific research suggests that our brains actively hear what we listen for.[3] We build on prior knowledge, both conscious and unconscious. The bottom line is that because we are clever, we struggle to be good listeners.

Part of being a good listener, then, involves consciously switching off this active or 'noisy' part of our brain. In *Dialogue: The Art of Thinking Together*, William Isaacs highlights this when he quotes the Indian philosopher Krishnamurti:

If we try to listen, we find it is extraordinarily difficult, because we are always projecting our opinions and ideas, our prejudices, our background, our inclinations, our impulses; when they dominate, we hardly listen at all to what is being said. In that state, there is no value at all. One listens, and therefore learns, only in a state of attention, a state of silence, in which this whole background is in abeyance, is quiet; then, it seems to me, it is possible to communicate.

Of course, switching off our own thoughts and finding this place of true silence to listen well is difficult. In *Deep Listening*, Oscar Trimboli explains why:

There's a gap between what you hear and what your mind can process. We speak between 125 and 175 words per minute, yet we listen to more than 400 words per minute. That means that no matter how fast they speak, your mind can process three to four times more words. It's this gap that causes you to drift off and be distracted ... our mind will drift or wander, and we'll often have the urge to interrupt midway through the conversation.

Being an effective listener is not a permanent state of being. It requires intention and focus, and it's very easy to lose the plot. But it's critical for us as leaders – and parents – to be highly effective listeners to build trust, develop relationships and facilitate great outcomes. Unless you consciously choose to listen deeply, the default position is to listen selectively to prove your existing theories.[4]

If you want an example of someone who listens to respond rather than empathetically or deeply, tune into your local radio station 'shock jock'. My 'favourite' used to be the recently retired Australian broadcaster Alan Jones, but you have plenty to choose from. Alan was infamous for talking over the top of his guest if they disagreed with his views. If you agreed with him, you'd get plenty of airtime. Otherwise, he would interrupt, challenge and close down alternative points of view. His listening style did little to facilitate genuine dialogue – rather, it created or compounded conflict.[5]

You might think it's fine to exhort the importance of listening, but in the real world, when you're having a tough conversation, it all goes out the window. This can be true, but when you begin to focus on practising your skills, you do listen better under pressure.

Occasionally, I have clients who express concern that if they listen empathetically, the other person will assume they agree with them when in fact they don't. To address that situation, simply say something like, 'I'm not sure I agree with what you're saying, but I'd like to understand your perspective. Can you please tell me more?' This way, you make your position clear but can still listen attentively.

How good a listener are you?

Give yourself a score on each of the following questions from 1 to 5. Use the following ratings:

1 = Never, 2 = Rarely, 3 = Sometimes, 4 = Often, 5 = Always.[6]

Do you	1	2	3	4	5
Bring a genuinely curious mindset to the conversation?					
Suspend your inner thoughts and give your undivided attention to the other person when they are speaking?					
Give the speaker plenty of time to talk and reflect?					
Allow people to finish their sentences without interrupting?					
Look at the speaker with encouraging eye contact?					
Listen to both the verbal content and non-verbal cues using all your senses? (Eyes, ears, heart)					
Smile at the speaker and lean forward with genuine interest?					
Pause and reflect before responding to what has been said?					
Demonstrate you have understood what has been said by summarising or paraphrasing?					
Invite the speaker to tell you more to gain a deeper understanding?					
Breathe slowly to manage your own emotions and inner thoughts?					
Ask questions that open up the discussion and draw out emotion as well as fact?					
Create an atmosphere of trust and connection through listening?					
Avoid 'fake listening' or 'listening just for show'?					
Avoid fidgeting with objects, or looking at your watch/phone?					
Acknowledge the speaker's feelings and demonstrate empathy?					

To get a wider perspective on how well you listen, you might want to ask colleagues, friends, family and maybe even clients to complete the preceding survey (about you) to learn their opinions of your listening practices.

Becoming a better listener

We can all improve the quality of our listening. I set out below a series of actions that will help.

Think about what you do now

How good a listener are you? Take the quiz provided in the preceding sidebar to identify opportunities to improve. Ask friends, colleagues and family to complete the quiz (about you) to get some feedback on how they experience you as a listener.

Listen to yourself

When we think about listening, the focus is on the other person – the speaker. However, to become a better listener, the starting point is to become better at listening to yourself. Being conscious of what you are thinking and feeling can help you manage the conversation.

In *Difficult Conversations*, Stone, Patton and Heen state, 'Only when you are fully aware of your own thoughts can you begin to manage them and focus on the other person.' And in *Deep Listening*, Trimboli notes, 'You need time to tune in and recognise what is running through your own mind, then clear away this clutter and create a space to make room to hear others.' Using the self-reflection framework (outlined in chapter 3) is a great way to do this.

Bring a curious and respectful mindset

Have a genuine interest in understanding the other person's perspective. According to Stone, Patton and Heen in *Difficult Conversations*, 'Listening is only powerful and effective if it is authentic. Authenticity means you are listening because you are curious and because you care, not just because you're supposed to.'

People respond positively when they think you are genuinely interested in understanding the situation. Asking great open questions and listening respectfully to what they have to say helps. Asking: 'Please tell me more,' or 'What else?' will often also reveal useful information. (I spend some time on what open questions look like shortly.)

Listen to the content

One of the simplest ways to keep your focus during a conversation is to listen to what the other person is saying and summarise or paraphrase it back to them. For example, you can use phrases such as, 'So my understanding of what you're saying is ...' or 'What I'm hearing you say is ...' By doing this, you demonstrate you've heard and understood what they've said. If you get the summary wrong, they have the chance to correct you and ensure you get back on track. As Stone, Patton and Heen note in *Difficult Conversations*, once people feel heard, they are significantly more likely to listen to you. Part of listening to the content is managing your desire to interrupt before the other person finishes speaking. By summarising periodically during the conversation, you help to keep this very human behaviour in check.

Listen for meaning

Besides listening to words, you need to be listening more broadly with all your senses. Look for the hidden meaning. Non-verbal cues, such as facial expressions, tone of voice and body language, will often provide you with more information about what someone is saying or not saying than the words themselves.

For several years, I've been part of a coaching supervision group with several outstanding coaches. I'm often amazed by their ability to pick up the hidden meaning in our conversations. They'll pick up one word, a pause or a movement and gently explore the issue, often identifying something far more meaningful.

Listen for, and acknowledge, feelings

Feelings crave acknowledgement. I was coaching two executives, Sarah and James, who needed to work closely together. The relationship broke down following a disagreement on an important decision. During our joint coaching, one thing was stopping progress. Sarah felt James was failing to acknowledge that her perspective was reasonable. James just wanted to move forward, but Sarah was stuck. She had been hurt by his comments and apparent unwillingness to recognise that she had acted reasonably and with good intent. She needed James to acknowledge this. Only when James finally acknowledged her feelings and apologised, did she became fully engaged. Because at that point, she felt he cared.

Listen for the emotions behind the words. Saying things like, 'I'm getting a sense you're unhappy with my response' or 'It sounds like you're frustrated with the situation' can often shift the conversation. When you acknowledge the other person's feelings, they perceive you care about them. And even if you misinterpret their emotional state, they'll still appreciate your effort to understand how they are feeling.

Breathe

Taking a slow, deep breath helps you keep your composure and focus, which is critical when you're trying to listen. When you're in a conversation, make it a practice to take slow deep breaths periodically to nourish your brain and stay in the moment. (Obviously, you need to do this discreetly, so you don't interrupt the flow of conversation.)

Value and leverage silence

Skilled listeners leverage pauses and silence in conversations. They don't immediately rush to share their own thoughts or ask a question, but instead hold back and give the other person the chance to reflect and add to what they have already said.

In *Deep Listening*, Trimboli again provides insight here, noting:

> The likelihood that someone can express an idea in their head completely, fully and effectively the very first time they speak is very low. Therefore, it's critical to understand that the pause, the silence, the breath – the moment when the speaker revisits what they haven't fully expressed – isn't the time for you to jump in and ask a question that will help contrast your perspective or create a new path in the discussion.

Being comfortable with silence is invaluable. It gives people a chance to reflect and refine what they want to say.

Ask great open questions (with care)

Part of effective listening is asking great open questions. This needs to be done carefully, and I explore this in more detail later in this chapter.

Practise and seek feedback

Listening effectively is a challenge. It's hard to suspend your ability to think ahead and solve problems, to block out self-talk and to stay focused on listening to what the other person is saying. The simplest way to get better is to practise and get feedback. Every day, you will be able to practise effective listening. Pick one conversation each day and try to use the skills identified through this section. Find people you trust and feel comfortable with, and ask them, 'How well do you feel I was listening during our conversation? What's one thing I can do better to improve my listening?' (I spend more time on giving and receiving feedback in chapter 7.)

Listening well is challenging

You can't listen and solve the problem in your head at the same time. And listening when you're feeling under attack and your amygdala comes into play is hard. You must practise suspending your own thoughts and tuning into the other person. Every day, you will get plenty of opportunities – at home and work – but to improve, you need to focus and practise.

ASKING GREAT OPEN QUESTIONS

Earlier in this chapter, I talk about bringing a curious mindset to hard conversations. By being curious, you listen in a way that shows you care. One way you can show your genuine curiosity is by asking great open questions.

Great open questions allow you to explore – to mine for information. They enable you to move from confusion to understanding. Great open questions invite participation. They give permission for the other person to share their perspective in a safe environment, which can change the dynamic of the conversation. Often, a defensive and adversarial dynamic will shift to something vastly different and more collaborative – a dialogue where parties create meaning and identify solutions together.

Let me share a story to illustrate the point. Katrina, a client of mine, was confused, frustrated and angry. Michelle, who headed Katrina's team, had promised Katrina that they would allocate the next major project that came into the office to her. When the next two new projects were given to other people, Katrina was not happy. She told me that Michelle didn't like her and was abusing her power. Katrina said nothing directly to Michelle, but was telling everyone who'd listen that Michelle was vindictive and untrustworthy. I suggested to Katrina that it was probably worth reminding Michelle of their conversation and asking her what had influenced the decision to give the projects to the other team members.

She took my advice. It turned out that one of the firm's clients had specifically requested a person for the first project, while the CEO had directed Michelle to give the second project to an interstate office, because they needed the work. While it would have been helpful for Michelle to have shared this information earlier, by not asking the question, Katrina jumped to an incorrect conclusion and increased her anxiety. The next big project went to Katrina.

In *The Fearless Organization*, Amy Edmondson highlights the importance of leaders asking what she calls 'genuine' questions to create psychological safety in the workplace. She states:

> Genuine questions convey respect for the other person – a vital factor for psychological safety ... Moreover, when asked thoughtfully, a good question indicates to others that their voices are desired – instantly making that moment psychologically safe for offering a response.

Isaacs also talks about the importance of good questions in *Dialogue*:

Instead of good answers, we need good questions. The power of dialogue emerges in the cultivation, in ourselves, as well as in others, of questions for which we do not have answers. Identifying one good question can be vastly more significant than offering many partial answers.

Learning how to ask open questions does not happen overnight. Early in my coaching career, I found it hard to move from asking closed questions (which invite yes/no answers) to open questions, but I worked at it. I'd begin to ask a closed question, stop myself and reframe it. It took time, but I got there in the end. (Though that's not to say I don't still occasionally muck it up.)

Of course, being able to ask brilliant open questions is only part of the game. Asking open questions at the right time is really what makes a difference. This, too, comes with practise and experience.

While asking questions can be transformative and valuable, questions can also be a double-edged sword. Effective listening is about encouraging the other person to speak freely and fully about their experience, without you interfering by agreeing, disagreeing or directing. When you ask questions, you're directing the conversation, and this may not always be helpful. Sometimes your questions might impede discovering critical information or change the flow of the story unhelpfully. For example, someone might be about to share what they feel is a crucial piece of information but then you interrupt to ask them about something else. When this happens to you, how do you feel about the interruption? Frustrated? Disrespected? In these cases, it makes sense to hold back on directive questions until the other person feels heard. When I say directive, I mean anything beyond 'Tell me more' or 'What else?' Once the other person feels heard, they are much more likely to listen to your substantive questions and explore the issues.

As Stephen Covey says in *The 7 Habits of Highly Effective People*, 'First seek to understand, then be understood.' Effective listening is like baking a cake. You need the right ingredients and the right timing. Too many questions or questions asked at the wrong time will not give you a good outcome.

A final observation: the tone you use when asking questions will have an enormous impact on how the other person receives the question. Questions asked with a tone of genuine curiosity will be received differently to questions asked with smug condescension!

Open versus closed questions

Asking questions helps you understand what is going on for the other person. They will feel heard and be more likely to listen to you. As discussed in chapter 3, in hard conversations, the best questions are usually 'open-ended questions' – questions that begin with who, what, when or how. They invite expansive responses, in contrast to 'binary' or 'closed' questions, which stimulate 'yes/no' responses.

For example, a binary or closed question would be, 'Is it raining?' In contrast, an open question would be, 'What's the weather like?' This gives rise to a far broader range of responses. Closed questions also have an important role to play, especially when you're seeking to clarify and confirm. Open, exploratory questions, however, are usually the key to gaining insight and understanding.

Be careful of why

While beginning a question with 'Why' does create an open question and is useful when you're researching or doing root cause analysis, it can be dangerous in hard conversations.

As I talk about in chapter 3, when asked 'Why?' people often feel like they are being blamed and they immediately go on the defensive. 'Why did you take that action?' is often interpreted as 'Why did you do that, you idiot?' and triggers a defensive response. This question is better framed using who, what, when, where or how. You get to explore the same issue without the risk of a defensive response. Instead of, 'Why did you take that action?', for example, you could ask, 'What influenced your decision to take that action?' This is less judgemental and more likely to generate a constructive conversation. In addition, your tone is less critical.

In chapter 3, I refer to the work of Sherod Miller that is helpful when trying to self-reflect and perspective take. By looking at each of the areas in Miller's framework to identify what you don't fully understand, you can come up with some great open questions. These questions not only get you information, but also cause the other person to feel you are genuinely interested in what they have to say.

Useful open questions

Some examples of useful open questions include the following.

Questions about sensory data:

- What have you seen or heard that I need to understand?
- What are people saying about the situation?
- What's happened that I should know about?
- What did your boss/colleagues/client tell you?

Questions about the other person's thoughts:

- What are you thinking about the situation?
- What were you thinking when you did *x*?
- What were you expecting?

- What did you assume would happen?
- What do you think is reasonable/unreasonable here?
- This is how I see the situation ... How do you see it differently?
- What do you think we should do?
- Tell me what you think about my decision.

Questions about 'emotions':

- It seems like you are unhappy, concerned [and so on] about ... Am I reading this correctly? (I know that this is a closed question, but in this context, it works like an open question, because it invites a broader response.)
- How are you feeling about the situation?
- What emotions are coming into play for you here?
- Tell me, what's going on for you?

Questions about 'actions':

- What have you done to deal with the situation?
- How might your actions (or inaction) have contributed to the situation?
- What are you doing now, and is that helping?
- What might you do to resolve the situation?

Questions about 'wants':

- What do you want most?
- What do you want to avoid?
- What don't you want?
- What do you want for the business/other stakeholders?
- What is really bothering you?
- What do you want from me?

If you feel uncomfortable asking questions in conversations, try thinking about areas of common ground and start there. When talking to your boss, for example, you might ask, 'What do you see as our biggest challenges over the next few months?' When talking to a team member, you might ask, 'What would you like to become better at that would help your career?'

Sometimes you might find you're in a conversation with someone who just won't stop talking. It's hard to get a word in – let alone a question. When this happens, a great open question can help. It'll stop them in their tracks because they'll actually have to think. If you know you're going to be dealing with someone like this, spend some time thinking about a couple of questions that go to the core of the issue before you catch up with them. Of course, closed questions (with yes/no answers) can be very helpful when you have a super chatty person. They allow you to direct the conversation to an end game.

Alternatively, you might have a conversation with someone who just doesn't respond at all. Their modus operandi is almost monosyllabic responses. 'I'm fine.' 'Good.' 'Okay.' 'Not sure.' Great open questions can shift them, so they respond in a more meaningful way.

Practising your questioning capability

Think about another challenging conversation that you've had in the past (other than the one you used in chapter 3) or a challenging current scenario. Refer to the various examples of questions listed in this section and try to come up with five open questions that you wished you'd asked, or would like to ask.

SPEAKING WITH CLARITY

When you're trying to communicate effectively, you need to speak with clarity and confidence. This is the final skill I focus on in this chapter.

Expressing your voice isn't enough. You need to do so in a way that enables the other person to understand what you have to say. In their 'Becoming Conflict Competent' course, Miller, Runde and Flanagan suggest that speaking with clarity is essentially made up of six components:

1. speaking for yourself (owning your comments)
2. describing your sensory data (what you see/hear)
3. expressing your thoughts
4. sharing your emotions
5. disclosing your wants
6. owning your actions.

By bringing all these components into the conversation, you create the clarity needed for effective communication.

Speaking for yourself (owning your comments)

The concept of speaking for yourself might sound strange. You may think, *Well if I'm talking, of course I'm speaking for myself!* But if you listen to people speaking, you discover they don't always own what they are saying. If you're old enough, you may remember the British Comedy series *Yes Minister*. In the show, the Minister has a permanent secretary of the department called Sir Humphrey Appleby and a private secretary called Bernard Woolley. Sir Humphrey and Bernard would rarely say what they thought, creating great confusion for the Minister. For example, instead of saying, 'I don't think that would be a good idea', they would say, 'Some people might not like that idea'. The Minister was constantly seeking further explanation, because he never understood exactly what the speaker was saying. (Of course, many current politicians have also been accused of such double-speak.)

Or, instead of owning what they have to say, people will revert to the language of judgement. Rather than saying, 'I'd like you to try this approach', they say, 'You shouldn't use that approach'. Right, so what should I do?

To speak for yourself, you need to use pronouns such as 'I', 'me' or 'mine' when framing a message. For example:

- 'I was thinking that ...'
- 'I noticed you paused when I asked you to ...'
- 'My concern is that ...'

Owning the content and speaking in this manner reduces confusion.

Table 4.1 illustrates some further examples of the contrast between judging comments, speaking for no-one and speaking for yourself.

Describing your sensory data

By sharing specific information, you make it easier for the other person to understand your perspective. Using concrete examples takes away ambiguity, and provides clarity and evidence to support what you have to say. If you do not provide the data, people tend to push back and dismiss your perspective.

Sharing your 'observations' is very different from making a judgement or an evaluation. In *Nonviolent Communication*, Marshall Rosenberg notes that when people make an evaluation (rather

Table 4.1: Examples of judging comments, speaking for no-one and speaking for yourself

Judging/evaluation	Speaking for no-one	Speaking for self
You shouldn't do that	It might be good to consider this.	I'd like you to try doing it this way.
It's bad that you've been late for the last two team meetings. Lift your game.	Some people might be upset at you arriving late to our team meetings.	I'm unhappy you have arrived late for the last two meetings. I really value your contributions and I'm also concerned that your conduct doesn't support our team value of respect.
You are letting the team down/ Your behaviour is disappointing.	Other members of the team may feel unhappy with your conduct.	I want you to be an effective member of the team. It upsets me when you fail to do what you say you will do.
You are a rude, inconsiderate person.	Some people are suggesting you are rude and inconsiderate.	I felt upset and disrespected when you interrupted me and then spoke over the top of me at this morning's meeting.
You need to be more careful.	There is some concern about your approach to risk management.	My concern is that this decision will affect a lot of people. I'd like you to give it some further consideration to ensure it is the best decision for the business.

than an observation), the other person responds differently. When people hear an evaluation, they hear criticism and resist what you are saying. When they hear an observation, they are more likely to listen and take it on board. Using specific data helps move the statement away from evaluation and towards observation.

Table 4.2 shows some examples of evaluation versus observation statements.

Table 4.2: Examples of evaluation and observation statements

Evaluation	Observation (data)
'You're always late.'	'I've noticed you arrived at least 15 minutes late to three of our last four team meetings.'
'Customers are unhappy with your work.'	'The report identifies 12 specific customer complaints in relation to your work.'
'You don't like me, do you?'	'I noticed you frown and shuffle your feet when I announced my decision.'

Expressing your thoughts

Saying what you think or believe often helps the other person comprehend the situation. By outlining your expectations and assumptions, you make it easier for the other person to grasp where you are coming from – for example:

- 'Given the size of the order and the timeline, I believe we will struggle to meet the deadline if we don't get more resources.'

- 'After reading the report, I'm assuming that customers will not accept the inferior product.'

- 'Considering the number of complaints, I don't think your performance is meeting expectations.'

Sharing your emotions

If you're trying to communicate clearly, disclosing some of your emotions to the other person is often useful. I am not advocating you share all your emotions but, as I discuss in chapter 2, selective sharing of emotion can be helpful. For example:

- 'I'm concerned that we've left it too late.'
- 'I'm feeling frustrated that we're running behind schedule.'
- 'I'm excited by the opportunity, but we need to be careful.'
- 'I'm disappointed that we find ourselves in this position.'

Sharing your emotion has two benefits. First, the research makes it clear that naming an emotion can help you calm down. Second, when you share your emotional state with the other person, you help them understand where you are at. They gain insight and see you as authentic.

Disclosing your wants

Disclosing what you want for the business, yourself, the other person and stakeholders has several benefits. It enables people to understand where you are coming from and helps to eliminate the common perception that there is a hidden agenda or bad intent. It demonstrates your honest intent and, in doing so, builds trust.

Examples of disclosing your wants include:

- 'I want the group to achieve our KPIs.'
- 'I want you to be able to influence the final decision.'
- 'I want you to be successful and enjoy your role.'
- 'I don't want to be seen as negligent.'

Being open about what you want can help the other person see the common ground and creates opportunities for solutions.

Owning your actions

By stating your past, present and proposed future actions you demonstrate honesty, accountability and commitment.

Some examples of owning your actions in this way include:

- 'I realise I should have talked to you about this sooner and my failure to do so has created some confusion.'

- 'I'm currently liaising with Peter to explore alternative approaches.'

- 'I'll review the situation and come back to you tomorrow.'

Owning your past behaviour, being clear about what you are currently doing and spelling out what you intend to do builds trust.

Finding your voice in some situations can be confronting. When you lack positional power or the other person has an intimidating presence, silence is the simple way out. But silence often comes at a cost – a sense of disappointment that you didn't speak up, or a sense of resentment that bubbles away inside. Sharing your perspective can be scary and it takes courage. But with good preparation and practice, speaking with clarity can become a standard part of your toolkit.

In the next chapter, I take a deeper dive into how you prepare for hard conversations. I outline two different scenarios – one dealing with having a hard conversation with your boss and the other covering having a hard conversation with someone who reports to you – and look at how you can prepare for each of them.

Key points

- Having hard conversations requires the application of six core skills:

1. staying calm
2. self-reflecting
3. perspective taking
4. listening under pressure
5. asking open questions
6. speaking with clarity.

- Eight actions to help you stay calm during hard conversations are:

1. preparing for the conversation
2. practising breathing control techniques
3. practising mindfulness regularly
4. being conscious of your triggers
5. being curious
6. being aware of your physical responses
7. naming your emotions
8. breathing in the moment.

- Listening well is the foundation for effective communication. To become a better listener:

  - Think about what you do now and identify opportunities to improve.

  - Listen to yourself – clear your head to more effectively listen to the other person.

  - Bring a curious and respectful mindset to the table.

  - Listen to the content.

  - Listen for meaning.

  - Listen for, and acknowledge, feelings.

  - Breathe to stay calm.

  - Value and leverage silence.

- Ask great open questions.
- Practise your listening skills and seek feedback from people you trust.

• Keep in mind the following about asking open questions:

- One way we show our curiosity is by asking great open questions – who, what, when, where, how?

- Open questions facilitate psychological safety and allow you to gain insight and understanding.

- Great open questions will often shift a defensive and adversarial dynamic to something more collaborative and productive.

- Asking questions at the right time is important and comes with practice and experience.

- Questions can be a double-edged sword. Sometimes your questions can impede discovering critical information or change the flow of a story unhelpfully – so questions need to be used with discretion.

- Closed questions (which elicit yes/no responses) can be useful to clarify you have understood a message, but are less helpful when you are trying to elicit information.

- Be careful of using why questions – people often feel they are being judged or blamed when you use why. Try using what, when or how instead.

- Recognise the importance of tone when asking your questions – people react to tone as well as content!

• To communicate effectively you need to speak with clarity and confidence. Speaking with clarity involves six components:

1. speaking for yourself (owning your comments)

2. describing your sensory data (what you see/hear)

3. expressing your thoughts

4. sharing your emotions

5. disclosing your wants

6. owning your actions.

Action for right now

You can begin the march to the 10,000 hours needed to become an expert in hard conversations. While you are probably time-poor, as a leader, you will have many opportunities to refine your skills daily.

Stay calm and practise the breathing exercise in this chapter; be conscious of your own physical reactions when emotions kick in and take a slow, deep breath before responding.

Focus on your listening skills. Take the listening survey in this chapter once a month to help you stay focused on some of the key behaviours for effective listening. Consciously focus on listening at least once a day during a conversation.

Bring a curious mindset into the conversations and ask, 'How are they seeing their position as reasonable?' Practise asking open questions to gain insight and understanding. Stop using 'why' and start using 'what' or 'how'. Practise reframing your questions.

To speak with clarity, practise saying what you really want to say by using all parts of the Circle of Self Reflection described in chapter 3. If you do this, you will save eons of time previously wasted in pointless and destructive conflict.

CHAPTER 5

Preparing for hard conversations: Two case studies

In chapter 3 I talk about the benefits of preparing for a hard conversation and outline a process that many of my clients have found useful. When you prepare properly, you increase the chance of the conversation being constructive, rather than going pear-shaped.

In this chapter, I examine two case studies to demonstrate how you can use this preparation process. (I've included the framework again in figure 5.1 as a reminder.) The first case study involves an example conversation with your boss, while the second scenario involves a conversation with a member of your team. By working through these two scenarios, you can become more familiar with the suggested approach and better able to apply the framework to your own challenging situations.

Figure 5.1: The six-step process for hard conversations

As mentioned in chapter 3, the preparation process involves you asking the following questions:

1. What is going on for me in this conflict? (Self-reflection)

2. What's going on for the other person? How can they possibly see it like that? (Perspective taking)

3. What would I like to understand? (Open questions)

4. What do we have in common? What do we both want? (Common ground)

5. What tough questions and objections do I need to be prepared for?

6. What are my key goals and messages for this conversation?

Over the past 13 years, I have used this framework with more than 2000 clients, and I can honestly say all but one found the framework useful (you can never please everyone). Like all good frameworks, it is not meant to be a straitjacket – rather, it is meant to provide a useful structure to navigate complexity.

Each of the case studies used in this chapter represents a blend of the many common scenarios I have worked on with clients. Names have, of course, been changed to protect the innocent.

The first case study imagines a scenario where you are a manager with a difficult boss – a managing-up conversation. Then I look at a scenario where you are the boss and find yourself having to talk to a problematic team member – a managing-down conversation.

SCENARIO 1: A TOUGH CONVERSATION WITH YOUR BOSS

You've been working at Simplexity, a highly regarded information technology business, for five years and have always received good performance reviews. You work hard and are good at what you do. For the first three years, you loved your job. You liked the organisation and the team culture that your old boss had created. You were given interesting and challenging work, and had a good working relationship with your boss. You caught up with her every two weeks and she would always make herself available when you wanted to bounce around tricky issues.

Two years ago, your boss left and one of your peers, Jackson, was promoted to act as your new manager. No-one asked you if you were interested in applying for the role and this bothered you a little, but you decided to let it pass and get on with the job. You had never worked closely with Jackson, but you had always gotten along reasonably well.

Jackson is a couple of years younger than you and doesn't have as much experience in some parts of the business. The first year went well and you received a good performance review from Jackson. But then things started to change. Where your old boss would always share the interesting work, Jackson began to keep the good stuff to himself. You found yourself being given the more boring, technical work that you are good at, but don't really like.

You have also noticed that Jackson seems to be leaving you out of senior management meetings that you had previously been invited to. You are beginning to think Jackson resents some of the relationships you have with senior people. You also think he's uncomfortable with your level of expertise. You attended a couple of meetings with him where he was asked questions he could not answer, and you found yourself stepping in. You sensed he did not like this.

Your willingness to challenge Jackson at team meetings does not seem to go down well either. On a couple of occasions he has talked over you or cut you off, which makes you think he just doesn't like you. The most recent occasion he did this was during last week's team meeting when you were trying to explain why you felt it made sense to change the way the team processed work requests.

You are keen to continue developing your career and expertise, because you'd like to get to the next level in the organisation. When you have raised this with Jackson, he says all the right things but has done nothing to help you. Recently, you became aware of a leadership development program being offered to people at your level and were told by someone in People & Culture that Jackson hasn't nominated you for the program. You feel disappointed and confused – you would love to do the program and don't understand why you haven't been nominated.

In addition, you have wanted to discuss a complex issue with Jackson on a couple of occasions, but he said he was too busy and that he was 'sure you could work it out yourself'. You've had to back out of one or two meetings with Jackson too, but you want to be able to meet with him more regularly to discuss work issues and get his input on some of your more complex problems. You don't understand why he seems to be resisting this.

You are starting to resent the way Jackson is managing you. You are no longer enjoying your job as much as you did before he became your boss, and you're concerned that your career is being stifled.

So, you decide to set up a meeting to talk things through.

The following outlines a hypothetical analysis for working through my process and framework.

1. Self-reflection: What is going on for you in this situation?

When you use the Circle of Self Reflection (refer to chapter 3) to try to make sense of the situation, you can jump from one part of the framework to any other. It's an iterative process – more like a pinball machine than a fixed step-by-step approach. However, for the purposes of working through the exercise, I'll go around the framework one segment at a time.

What you're seeing and hearing

What are you seeing and hearing in this situation? What are the facts?

- Your old boss and clients repeatedly telling you, 'You're doing great work; we love working with you.'

- The work you are getting from Jackson in the last 12 months has changed – you are getting a lot more technical work, but hardly any of the more interesting projects that involve you working with senior clients. Jackson is doing much of this work himself.

- Jackson saying, 'I want to help you develop your career.'

- Jackson going red in the face and looking flustered when you answered questions in meetings that he could not answer.

- You are no longer getting invited to meetings by Jackson that you previously attended together.

- Jackson has declined your meeting invites, saying, 'Sorry, I'm just too busy – I'm sure you can work it out for yourself.'

- Jackson has shown no interest in having regular one-on-one meetings.

- Jackson has talked over the top of you in meetings on at least three occasions – the most recent being during last week's team meeting when you were trying to explain why you felt it made sense to change the way the team processed work requests.

- A People & Culture colleague tells you about a new leadership development program and explains that, while Jackson was informed about the program, he hasn't nominated you.

What you're thinking

What are you thinking about the issue? What stories are you telling yourself? What are your assumptions and expectations? What values are coming into play?

- I'm great at my job and have a good work ethic.

- I should have been asked to apply for Jackson's role – I have more experience and would probably have done a better job.

- Jackson does not feel comfortable with me – he's a little insecure because he knows I know more about the business than he does, and I have strong relationships with senior managers.

- Jackson is hogging all the good work. He's being selfish – it's unfair!

- Jackson doesn't like me and doesn't really want me in the team – he's trying to get me to leave.

- Jackson has no interest in helping me develop my career.

- I expected that Jackson would want to continue to have fortnightly one-on-one meetings, like my old boss.

- Jackson is a very average manager and doesn't like being challenged.

- Jackson is not treating me with the respect I deserve.

- Maybe I'm being unfair and need to explore some of my assumptions and talk to Jackson?

- Maybe something is going on that I'm unaware of?

Feelings

How are you feeling about the situation? What emotions are coming into play? You might be feeling:

- angry
- confused
- disappointed
- frustrated
- uncertain
- unhappy.

Motivations

What do you want for the business/organisation?

- To be successful – meet our growth targets and other strategic objectives.

What do you want personally?

- To enjoy my job.
- To feel respected and valued.
- To grow and develop my career – and have a plan to make this happen.
- To have a good working relationship with my boss – regular one-on-one meetings and a commitment to have 'hot issues' meetings when we need to.
- To be given interesting and challenging work – a fair distribution.

What do you want for your boss (Jackson)?

- To feel he can rely on me.
- To succeed in his role and be respected by his manager and other leaders.
- To be happy with the team.
- To enjoy his role and be happy at work.

What do you want for other stakeholders such as clients and team members?

- I want the team to be respected and valued by our clients.
- I want our clients to be happy with the service we provide.
- I want the team to be happy and feel supported.

What you have done or are doing

What actions have you taken that might be relevant? What haven't you done?

- I may have been a bit distant with Jackson when he first got appointed.

- I have complained to others about not getting quality work and about Jackson's leadership.

- I haven't spoken to Jackson about my concerns.

- I cancelled a couple of meetings with Jackson at the last minute due to some personal issues.

- I often challenge Jackson in team meetings.

2. Perspective taking: How can Jackson possibly see it like that?

In this part of the process, you need to step back and try to look at the situation through the eyes of Jackson. Pretend you are Jackson when answering the following questions. Because I have not given you much information about how Jackson sees the situation, I'll be a bit creative and leave some areas blank. When you are doing this in real life, you will hopefully have better data to work with. For this scenario, I've called you Chris. To be clear, the hypothetical responses are your attempts to capture what you think your boss would say in relation to the various questions.

What you're seeing and hearing

What's Jackson's sensory data in this situation? What is he seeing and hearing? What are his facts?

- My boss is telling me ...

- Other members of the team are saying that Chris is complaining about me.

- Clients are saying …
- Chris is correcting me in front of clients.
- Chris regularly challenges me in front of the team.
- Chris cancelled at least three meetings we had set up in the first 12 months after I was appointed.

What you're thinking

What could Jackson be thinking about the issue? What stories is he telling himself? What could be his assumptions and expectations? What values are coming into play?

- Chris is a pain to work with – she can be quite arrogant and disrespectful.
- Chris thinks she should have got my job – thinks she's better than me.
- Chris doesn't respect me and resents me – deliberately tries to show me up in front of clients and the team.
- I need to learn more about the business.
- Chris has a good work ethic and knows what she is doing.
- Chris has been getting more than a fair share of the more interesting work – I need to distribute the work more fairly among the team.
- I can rely on Chris to get things done.
- Chris wants to be left alone to get on with things. She doesn't want to be micromanaged.

Feelings

How is Jackson feeling about the situation? What emotions are coming into play? Jackson might be feeling:

- annoyed
- confused

- embarrassed
- excited
- happy
- hopeful
- overwhelmed
- stressed
- uncomfortable.

Motivations

What does Jackson want for the business/organisation?

- To be successful – meet our growth targets and other strategic objectives.

What does Jackson want personally?

- To enjoy my job.
- To be and be seen as a capable and fair leader.
- To be successful in my career.
- To be respected and valued by my boss, my team and our clients.
- To create a great team – a team that works well together and delivers great results to our clients.
- To have good working relationships with everyone in my team.
- To have a good working relationship with my boss.
- To do interesting and challenging work.
- For Chris to treat me with respect and not embarrass me in front of others.
- For Chris to stop talking about me behind my back.

What does Jackson want for Chris?

- To feel valued and respected.
- To progress her career and be successful.
- To be happy and feel part of the team.
- To enjoy work.

What does Jackson want for other stakeholders such as his boss, clients and team members?

- I want the team to be respected and valued by our leaders and clients.
- I want our clients to be happy with the service we provide.
- I want our business partners to speak positively about us.

What you have done or are doing

What actions has Jackson taken that might be relevant? What hasn't he done?

- I have stopped inviting Chris to the more interesting meetings because I was getting tired of her showing me up.
- I have decided to do more of the challenging work myself so I can increase my knowledge and understanding of the business.
- I have tried to share some of the more interesting work among the rest of the team.
- I have cut Chris off a few times during team meetings when she interrupts me or contradicts me.
- I forgot to nominate Chris for the upcoming leadership development program – I have just been snowed under.

3. Open questions: What would you really like to understand?

Having self-reflected and looked at things from Jackson's perspective, what questions might be useful to explore when you meet with Jackson? I'm not suggesting you ask all these questions, but the following examples give you something to work with. Here are some suggestions of what you might ask Jackson:

- 'How are you enjoying the role?'

- 'How do you think the team is going?'

- 'What is your boss saying about the team?'

- 'What feedback are you getting from our clients?'

- 'What do you see as our biggest challenges over the next few months?'

- 'What are your thoughts on my performance and how I'm going?'

- 'I've noticed I've been getting quite a lot of technical work lately and less of the more interesting work that I've previously done. I was wondering what was causing that?'

- 'I've noticed that you have stopped inviting me to the meetings with XYZ that I was previously attending. I haven't said anything previously, but this has been bothering me because I always enjoyed attending the meetings and felt it was good for my career. What caused you to make that call?'

- 'What are your thoughts on the best way for me to progress my career?'

- 'What areas do you think I need to develop?'

- 'What would be one thing I could do to make things better for you?'

- 'What else would you like me to do differently?'
- 'How do you think we could improve our working relationship?'
- 'I was thinking it would be useful if we caught up for an hour every two weeks to go through work and bounce around some of the trickier issues – how would that work for you?'
- 'What would be the best day and time to set up that meeting?'
- 'What do I need to do to make you more comfortable inviting me to the meetings with XYZ?'

4. Common ground: What do you have in common?

Quite a lot of common ground can be found here. You both want:

- the organisation to succeed
- the team to succeed and grow its reputation
- to be valued and respected
- work to be distributed fairly
- to have successful careers and build your own reputations
- your career to progress
- to have a good working relationship
- to have happy clients and stakeholders.

5. What tough questions and objections do you need to be prepared for?

Tough questions and objections can often be anticipated by using the perspective-taking exercise. In this situation, you might find Jackson saying some or all of the following:

- 'I've felt that you've made my life difficult from the time
  I started in the role.'

- 'Your behaviour in the meetings with XYZ has been quite
  disrespectful.'

- 'To be honest, the way you talk to me in front of the team is
  just rude.'

- 'You are quite arrogant.'

- 'Why do you think I stopped inviting you to the meetings?'

- 'You were getting way too much of the interesting work –
  it wasn't fair on the team!'

- 'Why don't you ever talk to me privately about issues? You
  seem to always wait to raise your objections in front of the
  team – I don't get it. It's embarrassing.'

- 'Others deserve to go on the leadership development program
  before you do.'

- 'I know that you talk about me behind my back. If you've got
  a problem, come and talk to me!'

Once you have identified the possible tough questions and objections, it's useful to think about how you might constructively respond. Table 5.1 shows some suggestions.

Table 5.1: Possible responses to questions and objections from Jackson

Question/objection	Possible response
You've made my life difficult from the time I started in the role.	That certainly hasn't been my intention. What have I done that's made you feel that way?
Your behaviour in the meetings with XYZ has been disrespectful.	That's disappointing to hear you say that. I haven't meant to be disrespectful. What have I done that causes you to say that?
To be honest, the way you talk to me in front of the team is just rude.	I don't mean to be rude. What do I do that you find rude?
You are really quite arrogant.	Oh, that's not something I want to hear. What am I doing that causes you to say I'm arrogant?
Why do you think I stopped inviting you to the meetings?	To be honest, I'm not really sure but I would like to understand. What caused you to stop inviting me to the meetings?
You were getting way too much of the interesting work – it wasn't fair on the team!	Oh. That surprises me. I thought the distribution I was getting under our old boss was pretty fair. What makes you say that?
Why don't you ever talk to me privately about issues? You seem to always wait to raise your objections in front of the team – I don't get it. It's embarrassing.	I really don't mean to embarrass you. I guess I just like to be open and honest. I've always been that way. I'm happy to hold back and discuss concerns with you later if you wish, but I think it's better to talk things out as a team. How would you like me to behave in future meetings?
Others deserved to be on the leadership program before you.	Oh, that's disappointing. I thought we had agreed you would send me on the next program. What other leadership development opportunities might be available for me if I can't attend this program?
I don't like you talking about me behind my back. If you've got a problem, come and talk to me!	Okay – fair enough. I'll make sure I don't do that in the future.

When you hear these objections, the idea is to take a breath, stay calm and explore. This will keep the temperature down and allow you to discuss the issues in a useful way. If you need to own your behaviour, own it. Try not to get defensive – rather, stay curious and explore the issue. Your job at this point is to try to understand why the other person thinks their comment is reasonable.

6. What are your key goals and messages?

With the benefit of working through the preceding steps, you can think about what you are trying to achieve in having the conversation. In this scenario, your key goals for the conversation might be to:

- understand Jackson's perspective
- clearly share your perspective and desired outcomes
- agree on specific actions to take things forward.

To achieve these goals, you will need to ensure you have clear messages that you can weave into the conversation. The messages will often be found in your Wants section of the self-reflection framework. In this scenario, you might want to communicate the following key messages:

- 'I want us to achieve our business objectives.'
- 'I want to support you and add value to the team – I want us to succeed.'
- 'I respect you and appreciate your expertise.'
- 'I'm confused about the change in work distribution.'
- 'I want to be challenged and grow my career.'

- 'I want us to have a great working relationship and meet more regularly.'
- 'I want a fair share of the interesting work.'
- 'I'd really like to go on the leadership development program and think I'm ready for it.'

The idea is not to use this as a script, but rather to clarify your thinking so you can be clear about the messages that are important to you. This will help you keep the conversation on track and keep things constructive.

Now let's take a look at a second scenario.

SCENARIO 2: A CONVERSATION WITH A 'PROBLEM' TEAM MEMBER

If you lead a team, at some stage you will inevitably need to have a hard conversation with one of your team members. The following scenario is common.

You now have a team of five direct reports. On any objective assessment, the team is not performing well. Your boss has made some pointed comments to you about the team's performance, expressing his surprise and disappointment that they have missed some key project deadlines. This bothers you because you have always been successful in your career and you have a great deal of pride in your work.

You are particularly unhappy with one member of your team – Vince. Vince is in his early 30s and has been with the organisation for three years. Previously, he worked in a different team. You recruited him into your team eight months ago after getting some good feedback about him from one of your colleagues, Ted (Vince's old boss), who had suggested Vince apply for the role.

As far as you are concerned, Vince has been letting the team down in the following ways:

- He is often late to meetings.

- He says he will do things and then fails to get them done within agreed deadlines.

- He always has an excuse when he fails to deliver on his promises – it's always someone else's fault.

- He is disruptive at team meetings. Sometimes he will sit there and not participate in any meaningful way, while at other times he will interrupt and talk over the top of people, creating a tense environment.

- One of the other team members has complained about Vince failing to do his share of the work and wants to know what you're going to do about it.

You do not like Vince's attitude and realise you need to have a conversation with him. This has been going on for too long and you have not done anything about it. You have been busy working on a special project for your boss and haven't had the chance to spend as much time with your team as you'd like. The regular one-on-one meetings that you planned to have with Vince and other members of the team have not happened.

You are about to meet with Vince to give him some feedback. You know you can be intense and have been told you can be a bit controlling. Why things haven't worked out better, however, is a bit of a puzzle, because you thought Vince would be great for the team. When you engaged him, you thought that his energy and experience with some of the new business processes would make the team more efficient. You know you have not been around as much as you would have liked, but you feel someone with his experience should be able to make decisions without you holding his hand. You set up a meeting to talk things through.

1. Self-reflection: What's going on for you?

Again, I'll go around the Circle of Self Reflection one segment at a time.

What you're seeing and hearing

What are you seeing and hearing in this situation? What are the facts?

- Ted saying, 'Vince is good. He'll add a lot of value to your team and I think he could learn a lot from you, which would be good for his development. I definitely recommend him.'

- Your boss saying, 'I'm surprised that your team is missing some key deadlines. It's making us all look bad. To be honest, it's very disappointing. I expected you'd be able to do the special project and keep your team on track. Now that you've finished the project, I expect you to turn this mess around.'

- Vince is often late to the fortnightly team meeting (he usually comes in at least five minutes after the meeting starts) and has missed at least two meetings over the last three months.

- Vince has missed two important deadlines without explaining why.

- Julie, one of your senior team members, saying, 'Vince is a pain and isn't doing his fair share of the work. What are you going to do about it?'

- In team meetings, you feel a lot of tension. Vince either stays quiet and fails to contribute or appears agitated and talks over the top of people (including you).

What you're thinking

What are you thinking about the issue? What stories are you telling yourself? What are your assumptions and expectations? What values are coming into play?

The following thoughts may be happening for you:

- I don't understand how this has happened. Ted told me Vince was good. I thought I could rely on Ted. I wonder if he was trying to get rid of Vince ...

- I thought Vince would be a great addition to the team – instead, he's created havoc.

- This makes me look like a poor manager. I didn't like Julie's tone when she spoke to me and asked me what I was going to do about Vince's behaviour. I can tell she's not happy with my leadership and that bothers me.

- This is bad for me and it's bad for the team.

- I hate disappointing my boss. I've never failed before, and success is important to me.

- Vince is unreliable and rude. I must deal with this – I need to be seen as doing my job as leader.

- I should have dealt with this sooner. Maybe I should have found a way to spend more time with Vince. I feel like I've let him down because I was spending so much time on the special project.

- I assumed Vince would fit in without any issues. Maybe there's more to this than meets the eye. Some of the older members of the team can be hard to deal with at times – they don't like change.

- I need to understand how Vince feels and sees things.
- I expected the team would welcome and support Vince – I wonder if they have?
- I wonder if Vince has understood his role and responsibilities.

Connecting what you're thinking to what you're seeing and hearing

When you capture a 'thought', it's useful to ask yourself, 'What have I seen or heard (that is, what's my sensory data) that's causing me to think this way?' In this scenario, you might think Vince is rude because of his behaviour in team meetings. If you haven't captured that behaviour, you can then add it to your data. This is important because when you are having the subsequent conversation, you will often need to share specific data to help the other person understand what you are saying.

Feelings

How are you feeling about the situation? What emotions are coming into play? You might be feeling some or all the following:

- angry
- annoyed
- concerned
- confused
- disappointed
- embarrassed
- frustrated
- guilty

- hopeful

- stressed.

When you identify an emotion, it's useful to ask yourself, 'What have I seen or heard (sensory data) that's causing me to feel this way?' (In the same way as it's useful to connect thoughts with sensory data – refer to the preceding sidebar.) In this scenario, you might feel embarrassed because your boss said he was surprised and disappointed. Making these connections will allow you to fully capture all of your sensory data.

Motivations

What do you want for the business?

- Success – I want to achieve our strategic objectives, business plan goals and KPIs.

- Have a high-performing team that delivers outcomes.

What do you want personally?

- To be a great leader (and be seen by others as a great leader).

- To continue to succeed in my career.

- To hit my KPIs.

- To be respected and trusted (by my boss, my team and our clients).

- For the team to collaborate well, enjoy working together and deliver great outcomes.

- Less stress.

- Vince to step up and achieve his potential – and stop disrupting meetings.

- To understand what's going on for Vince and the other members of the team.

What do you want for Vince?

- To enjoy his role and be happy at work, and to feel safe.
- To feel he is a valued member of the team.
- To be successful and grow.

What do you want for other stakeholders?

- Happy boss, happy CEO, and happy customers and clients.
- Happy team – for the team to feel valued, recognised, supported and rewarded, and to enjoy coming to work.
- For the team to be successful and hit their KPIs – and to feel like they are making a difference and are working as a high-performing team.

What don't you want?

- Vince to continue behaving as he is.
- The current tension within the team to continue.
- To fail as a manager and leader.

What you have done or are doing

What actions have you taken that might be relevant? What haven't you done?

- Spoken to Tim to evaluate Vince – relied on his recommendation.

- Talked to Vince about the role and shaped his expectations that he would be an agent for change, and that he would be meeting with me regularly to get support.

- Prioritised the special project over the team and cancelled many one-on-one meetings with Vince and other members of the team.

- Failed to provide Vince with regular support and mentoring.

- Failed to raise my concerns with Vince earlier.

- Appointed Julie as the second-in-charge.

- May not have clearly shared my vision and thinking around Vince's role and responsibilities with Julie and the rest of the team.

2. Perspective taking: What's going on for Vince?

Now you can try to look at the situation from Vince's perspective. Pretend you are Vince when answering the questions. Again, because I have not given you much information about how Vince views the situation, I'll be a bit creative. When you are doing this in real life, you will hopefully have better data to work with – though sometimes you won't. Don't be concerned if you struggle with this perspective-taking exercise, because this will highlight what you don't know and help you identify some of the questions you might wish to explore when you have the conversation.

In this scenario, I'll again call you 'Chris' so when 'Vince' talks about you he will refer to Chris (his manager).

What you're seeing and hearing

What's Vince's sensory data in this situation? What could he be seeing and hearing? What are the facts?

- My old boss (Tim) told me about the role in Chris's team. He said, 'It would be a great opportunity and you will learn a lot from Chris.'

- Chris told me about the role and explained, 'Our team needs to evolve and your skills and experience will be invaluable. I'll be meeting with you regularly to make sure you get plenty of support.'

- Others in the team were often critical of my suggestions when I sought to improve processes or ways of working – telling me to 'calm down', 'stick to the program', or saying, 'We don't do it that way here'.

- Chris apologising and pulling out of scheduled meetings (numerous times).

- Team members not responding to my emails or being slow to respond to urgent requests.

- Team members heading out to coffee/lunch/drinks and not inviting me to join them.

- Team members ignoring my requests for information that I needed to complete reports.

- Chris talking over me (and others) during team meetings.

What you're thinking

What could Vince be thinking about the issue? What stories is he telling himself? What could be his assumptions and expectations? What values are coming into play?

- This is not what I expected. I should never have left my old job. I should talk to my old manager about going back. This team sucks. They don't treat me with respect. They're trying to shaft me.

- I don't know why my old manager suggested I take this role.
- I thought the new team would welcome my ideas and be receptive to suggestions that improved processes. I was wrong!
- I expected to be supported as I gained an understanding of the role and projects.
- I thought I'd be welcomed and given decent training where necessary – that didn't happen.
- I don't feel like I'm a part of this team.
- I expected to be supported by Chris and that we'd meet regularly, as promised. That was part of the appeal of the role.
- Chris does not care about me. She is the worst manager I have ever had.
- The team don't like me. They resent me. There is no accountability in this team and they simply don't like change or being challenged.
- The team meetings are a waste of time. There is no agenda and no-one listens, including Chris, who is a control freak.
- I really do not like this role. I much preferred my old team.

Feelings

How might Vince be feeling about the situation? What emotions are coming into play? Vince might be feeling:

- confused
- disappointed
- frustrated
- hurt
- nervous

- overwhelmed
- stressed
- unhappy.

Motivations

What might Vince want for the business?

- To achieve strategic goals and deliver desired outcomes for clients and customers.

What might Vince want personally?

- To be respected, acknowledged and valued.
- To develop and learn, progress his career and make more money.
- Be part of the team – be valued, accepted, respected, heard and make a difference.
- Enjoy going to work – have a manager who acts as a mentor and coach.

What might Vince want for you (Chris)?

- Help my manager and my team to succeed – make you look good.
- Feel like Chris can trust and rely on me.
- Help Chris introduce new processes to improve efficiency and effectiveness.

What might Vince want for other stakeholders?

- Happy clients, happy teammates.
- Less admin and more time to do real work.

What doesn't Vince want?

- To be ignored, disrespected, not heard, excluded, bored and feel like I am not growing or learning.

- To work in a role that is unfulfilling and lacks meaning or to be neglected by my boss.

What you have done or are doing

What actions has Vince taken that might be relevant? What hasn't he done?

- Spoken at length to my old boss about the role with Chris's team and considered the pros and cons.

- Talked to other colleagues about Chris and her team.

- Agreed to take the role.

- Tried to tell the team how we could do things better.

- Tried to set up meetings with Chris to discuss issues I was having.

- Tried explaining the value of my suggestions to other members of the team.

- Lost my cool in a couple of team meetings.

- Have missed a few deadlines.

- Started to shut down – just not worth engaging.

3. Open questions: What would you really like to understand?

With the benefit of having self-reflected and looked at things from Vince's perspective, what questions might be useful to explore when you meet with Vince? Here are some suggestions:

- 'How are you finding the role?'

- 'What was your understanding of the role?'
- 'How has reality differed from your expectations?'
- 'How are you finding the team?'
- 'What are you finding challenging about the role or team?'
- 'What do you think we can do better as a team?'
- 'What learnings are there from your old team for us?'
- 'What would you like from me as your manager?'
- 'What support do you need that you haven't been getting?'
- 'How do you think you're going?'
- 'What do you think you can do better?'
- 'What might you do more or less of, or differently, to help the team improve?'
- 'What do you want to do, career-wise?'
- 'How can I help you develop?'
- 'What would you like me to do more or less of, or differently?'

4. Common ground: What do you both want?

Again, you have plenty of common ground to work with. You both probably want:

- to be successful and achieve organisational and team goals
- an effective team that achieves results and models organisational values – respect, trust and to enjoy work
- Vince to learn and grow – to progress his career and contribute to the team
- Vince to feel part of the team

- satisfied customers and stakeholders
- to build individual and team reputations
- to rebuild the relationship
- for the team to improve as a team.

5. What tough questions and objections do you need to be prepared for?

Tough questions and objections can often be anticipated by using the perspective-taking exercise. In this situation, you might find Vince saying some or all of the following:

- 'You are never around – it's very disappointing.'
- 'This role is not what you promised.'
- 'The team is hopeless.'
- 'No offence, but you are the worst manager I've ever had.'
- 'It's not my fault. How do you expect me to meet deadlines when people won't give me the information I need?'
- 'This is unfair.'
- 'I'm very unhappy and have been thinking about leaving.'

Once you have identified the possible tough questions and objections, you can think about how you might constructively respond. Table 5.2 shows some suggestions.

Table 5.2: Possible responses to questions and objections from Vince

Question/objection	Possible response
You are never around – it's been very disappointing.	I apologise for that. It's not something I planned, and I do intend to spend more time with you from now on.
This role is not what you promised.	I'm sorry to hear that you feel that way. I'm not quite sure I understand what you mean. What were you expecting that hasn't happened? What is happening that causes you to say that?
The team is hopeless.	Okay, that's not what I want to hear. What's happened that causes you to say that?
No offence, but you are the worst manager I've ever had.	All right, that's not what I want to hear. What have I done to cause you to reach that conclusion?
It's not my fault. How do you expect me to meet deadlines when people won't give me the information I need?	I don't want to play the blame game. I just want to understand what has been going on that's stopped you from meeting your deadlines. Please help me understand what's been happening.
This is unfair	Being fair is especially important to me. What do you feel is unfair?
I'm very unhappy and have been thinking about leaving.	I'm sorry you are unhappy. I want people to enjoy their work and I certainly don't want you to leave. I recruited you because I thought you'd be a great addition to the team. I want you to enjoy your job and be happy at work. What is causing you to be unhappy? What can we do to turn this around?

As I noted in the first scenario, when you hear these sorts of objections, the idea is to take a breath, stay calm and explore. This will keep the temperature down and allow you to discuss the issues in a useful way. If you need to own your behaviour, own it. Try not to get defensive. Rather, stay curious and explore the issue. Your job at this point is to try to understand why the other person thinks their comment is reasonable.

6. What are your key goals and messages?

With the benefit of working through the process, you can now step back and think about what you are trying to achieve in having the conversation. In this scenario, your key goals for the conversation might be to:

1. understand Vince's circumstances and perspective better, including issues, constraints and pressure

2. clearly explain your concerns, objectives and needs

3. agree on some specific actions to take things forward.

To achieve these goals, you will need to have some clear messages that you weave into the conversation. The messages will often be found in your Wants section when self-reflecting. In this scenario, you might want to communicate the following key messages:

- 'I'm sorry I haven't been available to provide you with more support.'

- 'I'm concerned about how the team is performing.'

- 'I want to talk to each member of the team to understand people's thinking.'

- 'I want us to become a more effective team.'

- 'I want to understand how you see things.'

- 'I want to explore how you are going in the role.'

- 'I value you as a member of this team and want you to enjoy your job.'

- 'I'd like you to step up in relation to how you behave in meetings and meeting deadlines.'
- 'I want to help you to learn and grow and be successful.'

Once again, the idea is not to use this as a script but rather to clarify your thinking – to prepare for the conversation. You want to be clear about the messages that are important. When you get pulled down a rabbit hole, these key messages can help you get you back on the path.

In the next chapter, I shift from preparation to actually having the conversation. I use the scenarios outlined in this chapter to demonstrate how you can use your preparation to navigate the conversation in the moment.

Key points

- In this chapter, I have used two case studies to illustrate how you can prepare for having a hard conversation. By taking time to plan and think through the situation, you can put yourself in a better position to be effective when you engage with the other person. Hopefully, these case studies will assist you when you apply the framework to your own challenging scenarios.

- While the first time you use this structure may take a little time, the experience of my clients is that once you have completed it two or three times, you can do it quickly – almost instinctively. The feedback I consistently get from my clients is that when they prepare well, the conversations go way better than they expect.

- Once you get used to doing this preparation for the conversations you can plan for, you will find that you will draw on the framework without thinking during unplanned conversations. In much the same way that Roger Federer instinctively plays tennis, you will instinctively pause, listen and ask great questions even when caught unprepared, which will inevitably lead to productive conversations.

Action for right now

To practise preparing for your own hard conversation, use the template provided in appendix B to ensure you are properly prepared.

CHAPTER 6

─────

Having the hard conversations: Two case studies

Musicians all over the world spend hours watching their favourite performers to pick up tips and hone their skills. Emerging athletes, similarly, spend many hours watching the superstars of their sport to emulate their skills and strategies.

While nothing replaces learning by doing, observing others performing a task is also useful. We learn from the things they do well, and from their mistakes.

In chapter 5, I explore how you might prepare for two hard conversation scenarios – the first relating to a situation with a difficult boss and the second involving a problematic member of your team. Preparing for a hard conversation increases the odds that you will handle it well.

In this chapter, I give you an opportunity to observe a manager who has prepared for each of the case studies from chapter 5, and is now having the hard conversations.

CASE STUDY 1: A HARD CONVERSATION WITH YOUR BOSS

As outlined in much more detail in chapter 5, this first scenario involves Chris, a member of a team who is having some issues with her former colleague Jackson, who has now become Chris's boss and team leader. Chris recognises the need to have a hard conversation and has arranged a meeting with Jackson to talk things through. To see how this scenario might play out in real life, I created an improvisation where I played the role of Chris and invited one of my colleagues to play the role of Jackson. The following is what took place.

Jackson: Hi, Chris. What's going on?

Chris: Hi, Jackson. Thanks for making the time to catch up – I know you're busy. I thought it would be useful to bounce around a few things that are going on and get your input, if that's okay?

Jackson: Okay, yep. Is this going to take long?

Chris: No, I don't think so. Probably about 20 to 30 minutes.

Jackson: Okay, let's go.

Chris: I wanted to start by offering an apology for cancelling our meeting last week at the last minute. I'm having some issues with my mother, who we've had to put in a nursing home. I realise it's important for us to meet regularly and I'm sorry I had to pull out.

By owning her behaviour, Chris reduces the tension.

Jackson: Thanks for that. It was a little frustrating – I wasn't sure what was going on. I'm sorry to hear about your mother.

Chris: Thanks – she seems to have calmed down and gotten used to the situation so hopefully things will be smoother from now on.

Jackson: That's good. So, what did you want to talk about?

Chris: There have been a few times in the last couple of months where I've sensed that you've been a little frustrated with me. I want to understand if I was reading you correctly.

Jackson: What specific situations are you thinking of?

Chris: On two or three occasions in meetings you've cut me off when I was contributing, and I had a sense that you were annoyed with me. I'm also a little confused why you've stopped inviting me to attend the monthly catch-up meetings with the senior managers. I've attended those meetings for the past two years and feel I make a valuable contribution. We haven't had a conversation about that, but I feel like something is going on that I need to understand.

Specific data helps Chris to illustrate her sense of frustration.

Jackson: I see. Okay, look, I wasn't really aware I was cutting you off in meetings. It's just that when I've been trying to articulate something or explain my position, you often seem to step in and contradict me. I know you've got some good experience in the business but, ultimately, I'm the decision maker, and that needs to be respected. It often feels like you are undermining me, to be honest, and I don't like it.

Chris: I'm really sorry that that's the impression you've been getting, because the last thing I want to do is undermine you. That's not how I work and it's not what I intended. I guess what was happening in those meetings was that, when I contributed, it was on the basis that I felt I was adding value. I certainly didn't intend to make you look bad.

Stating the good intent addresses the inference of bad intent.

Jackson: Well, that's good to hear. I am keen to get your input. You have got some valuable ideas, but you need to learn to temper the way you communicate. At times it just feels disrespectful.

Chris: Thanks. I appreciate your honesty. I just want to add as much value to the team and business as possible – and if I feel like I've got something to offer, then I do. But I guess maybe I need to give a little bit of thought to how I'm doing that.

Jackson: Yes I think that would be helpful.

Chris: What would you like me to do differently?

Jackson: I guess I'm just looking for a bit more respect, to be honest. I like your energy and want to leverage your experience. But it would be good if you could just let me finish expressing my thinking before jumping in. When you jump in, I can sometimes feel a bit overridden and challenged, I guess. Maybe you could let me finish and I'll then invite you to share your thoughts. Or, if I'm not sure of the answer, I'll invite you to share your thinking.

Chris's open question helps her gain insight and understanding.

Chris: Right, okay, that's fair enough. I know I can be a bit bullish at times. I'm very outcomes focused. I appreciate the feedback. I certainly don't want you to feel disrespected because I know that feels bad. To be honest, that's how I feel when you cut me off in our team meetings. And I guess I've felt a little disrespected when you stopped inviting me to the senior management meetings.

Chris acknowledges her contribution and then explains her perspective.

Jackson: Fair enough. Respect is a two-way street. We probably should have had this conversation earlier. I'll start looking to invite you to some of the meetings with senior managers again when I can see that your experience will add value.

By having the courage to gently push back, Chris gets a positive response.

Chris: That would be great. The other thing I'd like to talk about is the distribution of work within the team. I'm confused about what seems to be a change in the mix of work I'm getting. In the past, I did a lot of the more interesting and challenging strategic work. Lately, I've just been getting the more technical stuff that, to be honest, I don't enjoy. I know I'm good at it, but I don't enjoy it, and it's really affecting how I'm feeling about the job.

Jackson: I wasn't aware of that. I know that you have fantastic technical expertise and I see you as the go-to person on the complex tech stuff. When I want it done fast and done well, I think, Oh, great. I'll give it to Chris and I know that it'll come back in good shape.

Chris: I don't mind doing some of that work, but when it's the only thing I'm doing, it becomes a grind. It's not as stimulating as some of the other work that involves me working with senior managers on some of the more complex strategic issues.

Sharing emotions, data and thoughts in a constructive way results in a productive conversation.

Jackson: It wasn't really a deliberate decision. I suppose I was also wanting to make sure everyone got a good mix of work and that the work was being distributed fairly. I guess I have been giving you some of the more demanding technical work because I know I can rely on you, and I didn't appreciate how much this had changed the balance of your work. And I didn't realise it was having such an impact on you. Thanks for the feedback. What would you like to see happen?

Chris: I'd just like for things to go back to how they were before, in terms of having a more even distribution of work.

Jackson: I hear what you're saying. I'll be more conscious of making sure I give you a better mix of work in the future. We need to share the more interesting work around, but I will make sure you don't just get the technical stuff. When you feel that I've allocated you too many of those projects, just come back to me and say, 'Look, I've got too many of those technical projects on my plate at the moment. The balance is a bit out, so can you please allocate this to one of the other members of the team?'

Chris: Okay, I'm happy to do that.

Jackson: Is there anything else?

Chris: I also want to have a quick chat about the upcoming leader development program. I was hoping to be sent on the program this year and was wondering if you had given that any thought. I understand from the People & Culture team that the nominations need to come from you and that the deadline for the next program is coming up.

Chris effectively brings in her concerns and desires around personal development.

Jackson: Oh, yes, of course. I'd forgotten about the deadline. I've just got so much going on it dropped off my radar. I've also been approached by Julie about that program and I think only one spot is available for our team. Why do you think you're the right person to get the opportunity?

Discovers Jackson's workload rather than bad intent is the cause of the failure to nominate.

Chris: I think I'm ready for it and other people around the organisation think that I'm ready for it, according to some of the feedback I've gotten. I'm not saying that I should go ahead of Julie. I think we should both go on the program if possible. At the end of the day, I respect that you've got to make a call if you can only nominate one person. But I certainly think that, objectively, I would probably be put ahead of Julie in terms of who should go.

Chris reinforcing key message around respecting Jackson helps the conversation.

Jackson: Why would that be?

Chris: My experience and my understanding of the business. I think I'm ready to step up.

Jackson: Okay, here's what I'm going to do. I'm going to ask you and Julie to both provide me with a one-page document outlining three reasons you should go on the leadership program. I'll send both documents to People & Culture and will explore if I can get you both on the program. If I can only get one of you in the program, I'll make the call on who I think has made the strongest case. Obviously, I'll give you feedback on my decision and if you miss out, you can go next year.

Chris: Okay, that's fair enough. I just wasn't sure what was going on. If you think Julie's got a better case, then that's a fair call. I'll get that to you by the end of the week.

Jackson: Is there anything else?

Chris: The last thing I wanted to talk about was trying to lock in regular fortnightly catch-ups. I know I haven't helped things by cancelling a couple of meetings due to the stuff that has been going on with my mum, but I really do value the chance to bounce things around with you and would like to lock in a regular 45-minute fortnightly meeting in our diaries if that's okay.

Chris effectively brings in the key message around meetings and owns her contribution to the issue – which leads to a good outcome.

Jackson: That's fine. Can you talk to my executive assistant, and we can lock something in. Thanks for raising these issues today, Chris. It's been a good discussion. I'm under so much pressure all the time to deliver on what I've been asked to do, that it's often difficult for me to know whether people are happy or unhappy, because I'm just working so fast. So, thanks for taking the time to set it up and raise the issues with me. I feel like it's helped clear the air between us.

Chris: Thank you. I've appreciated your candour. I want to help in any way I can and I'll give some thought to what you had to say. Have a great weekend.

A nice way to end the conversation.

CASE STUDY 2: A HARD CONVERSATION WITH A PROBLEM TEAM MEMBER

The second conversation involves you as the team leader having a conversation with one of your team members, Vince. As detailed in chapter 5, you are unhappy with some of Vince's behaviour and performance, and have been asked by one member of your team what you are going to do about it. You don't understand why things haven't worked out with Vince, because he came highly recommended by one of your colleagues. The following is the improvised conversation. I played the role of the team leader and my colleague played the role of Vince. Again, the idea here is to illustrate how you put your preparation to use in an actual conversation.

Chris (team leader):	Hi Vince, thanks for coming today. I just wanted to bounce a few things around with you in terms of how you're going, your thoughts on the team, and what we might do to improve things generally. Does that sound okay?	*By setting context, Chris tries to reduce tension.*
Vince:	Sure. Is there something wrong?	
Chris:	Well, I've got an unhappy managing director reminding me that the team has missed a couple of important deadlines and KPIs. I've decided to talk to everyone in the team to try to get a sense of what people are seeing, feeling and hearing, and to come up with some ideas on how we turn this around.	
Vince:	Sounds reasonable.	
Chris:	I want to start by apologising for not being around as much as I had hoped to be. When you joined the team I told you that I would be spending time with you to make sure your transition into the team was smooth and that we could leverage your talent. Unfortunately, the project that I was asked to take on by the MD took a lot more time than I expected, and I know that my absence has affected the team.	

It's particularly affected you because you were new, and I know there are some tricky personalities. I want to apologise for that and let you know that the project's come to an end and I will be spending a lot more time with the team – and you – moving forward.

Offering an apology early can quickly defuse an issue that might otherwise hinder the conversation.

Vince: Thanks – that's good to know. It's been quite difficult, and it will be good to get more of your time. There are some real weaknesses in the team.

Chris: Okay. That's interesting, because I've always thought of it as a reasonable team. But we're not hitting our targets at the moment, so your observation has probably got some substance. I'd be interested in exploring your perspective a bit more, if that's okay. What do you see as the problems?

Acknowledging the point allows Vince to feel heard.

Vince: Where do I start? I don't think I've ever worked with a team that spent so much time grumbling and whingeing. We've got so much to get on with. But this group is caught up in a shitstorm of complaints and baseless tensions.

By being curious and asking open questions, Chris gathers lots of information and insight.

Chris: What are they complaining about?

Vince: They complain about everything – the workload, the way tasks are allocated, the deadlines being unrealistic and they push back on anything involving change.

Chris: Do you think their complaints have any substance?

Vince: Look, we do have some tight timelines, and some of the process changes I'm recommending can take a little time to get used to, but these guys just seem resistant to anything I suggest. They are completely different from my old team.

Chris: That's interesting – can you tell me more about the differences between us and your old team. I'm interested in what we can learn.

Vince: Well, I think the quality of the people in my old team was better – everyone had been trained to do their jobs and knew what they were doing. I don't mean to be critical, but a couple of people in this team seem completely out of their depth. And Julie's just a pain in the arse.

Chris: What do you think we can do to develop the skills that we need?

    Chris's question shifts Vince to a solutions mindset.

Vince: It's a tough one because we could try sending away those people to skill up, but that's going to put pressure on the rest of the team. I think we'd have to probably replace them in the interim.

Chris: Okay, I'll give that some thought. Now tell me what Julie has done to upset you.

Vince: She's just rude. She never listens to anything I say, she openly dismisses me in meetings, her attitude towards you is disrespectful, and she talks about me behind my back. She's toxic.

Chris: How are you getting on with the other members of the team? Is it just Julie or ...?

Vince: I get on okay with most of the team, but they all seem to follow Julie. If Julie resists something, they all just fall into line.

Chris: Okay. Going back to your old team, what else do they do differently that we can learn from?

After respectfully listening, Chris goes back to the issue she wants to explore.

Vince: Well, we ran our meetings very differently. We have been adopting the Agile approach to work, which is much more collaborative, so we all meet more often and share information. My old boss was big on giving everyone a chance to speak and we all knew what our priorities were and would help each other out. We worked as a team, not in silos, which is what I see around here. The Agile approach really improved the way we worked. I've been trying to introduce some of those practices, but Julie just tells me to pull my head in. It pisses me off.

Chris:	What would you like me to do?	*Great open question to engage Vince.*

Vince: I think you need to push back on Julie and look at shifting to Agile.

Chris: I was thinking about getting an external facilitator in to do some work on rebooting the team, maybe I should get someone who is familiar with the Agile methodology. What do you think?

Vince: I think that would be a good idea.

Chris: Thanks for your input on the team. I'll give what you've had to say some thought. I'd like to take a few minutes to talk about how you think you're going in the role if that's okay.

Chris explores the broader context (the team) before seeking permission to talk about Vince's performance.

Vince: Well, I know I'm good at my job. I know the work inside out. I think I'm doing fine. It's really just the team that's the problem for me.

Chris: Can I offer you some feedback?

Vince: Sure.

Chris: On a couple of occasions you have committed to delivering certain outcomes within hard deadlines and you've missed them. I didn't hear anything from you in terms of what was going on, whether you were going to miss the deadline or why. As a manager, I don't like surprises. If you've got some issues that are getting in the way, I need you to come and talk to me about them. I know I've been hard to get in touch with, but I do respond to my emails. And I want to know about any problems. I probably should have said something to you sooner but, moving forward, if you're looking like you're going to miss a deadline, can you let me know and help me understand why?

Chris provides specific data to enable Vince to understand the point.

By sharing her thoughts and emotions, and acknowledging she should have raised the issue earlier, Chris succeeds in getting Vince's buy-in.

Vince: Okay. Yeah, I can do that. But I can't do my job if people don't cooperate with me. If you can get the team to listen to my suggestions and respond to my requests, we'll make the deadlines. But until that happens, we're going to miss deadlines.

Chris: Okay, I'm committed to working to improve the team but, in the meantime, if you've got issues that are coming up, I'd like you to come to me and we can work through them to resolve them as we go.

By acknowledging the objection, Chris is able to return to the issue.

Vince: So, do you see this as my problem?

Chris:	I see it as a problem for all of us, but I think you've got a role to play. You've got to step up and let me know what's going on more often than you've been doing if you've got a problem.	*Providing a balanced response to the objection results in agreement.*
Vince:	Okay. Fair enough.	
Chris:	The other thing I wanted to talk about was your behaviour in our team meetings.	
Vince:	What do you mean?	
Chris:	I've observed some behaviour in team meetings that had me wondering what was going on. For example, in the last couple of meetings, I've watched you just withdraw and not participate at all, while on other occasions I've noticed you interrupting and talking over the top of Julie and then Greg. I want to know what's going on for you, because it wasn't exactly textbook behaviour.	*By sharing specific data and thoughts, Chris draws Vince into the conversation.*
Vince:	If I don't talk over the top of Julie in the meetings, she'll go on and on until we run out of time. She's such a pain.	
Chris:	I'll take some of the responsibility for that. I run the meetings and making sure everybody gets airtime can be hard. What I'm looking for from you is to model some of the leadership behaviour that we need. I think we need to talk more about how to deal with Julie,	*Chris clearly articulates what she wants from Vince behaviourally.*

because I know she is a challenge, but I don't want you interrupting her or talking over the top of her. And I do want you to participate and share your views.

By acknowledging Julie can be challenging, Chris draws Vince in.

Vince: I've never had this sort of problem before. In my previous teams, I haven't encountered this. We were all on the same page. We worked together and respected each other.

Chris: I think one of the benefits of coming into new roles is being challenged and stretched in ways that you haven't before. Without doubt, some people are harder to work with than others but, in terms of your own development, it's an opportunity for you to grow and develop. And part of my job is to help you do that.

Vince: Yeah, well, I'm just about ready to move on, to be honest, Chris.

Chris: Look, that's always an option, but it's not what I'd like. I'd like you to stay in this team because the reason I got you in was that you bring in expertise and experience that's going to be valuable for us. I'd like to work with you to make sure that we can push through some of these challenging issues within the team to create something better.

Chris spells out what she wants in a way that lands well.

Vince: I just feel like you've let me down, to be honest. You've just swanned back in after months of barely being around and now you're telling me I need to improve my behaviour. I don't know; it just feels wrong.

Chris: I can understand that frustration because I do recognise that my absence has contributed to the problem. But I think we've all got to own it – me, you, everyone in the team – and work towards rebuilding a great team. If nobody owns it, that's not going to happen. It's easy to walk away, but I don't think that that's the answer. I want to create a high-performing team, and having somebody like you in the team is going to be extremely helpful. While you could certainly leave the team, that's definitely not what I want to see.

Chris validates Vince's frustration and then reinforces key messages around everyone owning their behaviour, creating a better team and valuing Vince as part of the team.

Vince: So, what do you want me to do?

Chris: I'd like you stay and work with me to rebuild the team. As I mentioned, I'm looking to get an external consultant in who specialises in working with teams to help us.

Vince: I've been in these facilitation things before, and they are often a waste of time. We've got so much on, and with somebody as disruptive as Julie – I'm not confident that it's going to work.

Chris: I'll find somebody good and make sure
         they have a chance to talk to everyone
         before we meet, so we increase the
         chance of it being successful.

Vince: To be honest, this team just needs
         a big injection of positivity.

Chris: That's part of what I want to do with
         this external facilitator – give people
         a bit of room to see where we're at
         now, what we'd like to be and what the   *Chris*
         possibilities are. Then we can work   *acknowledges*
         through the processes for how we do   *the validity*
         that. That's not going to be easy, but I've *of the objection*
         seen it done before and colleagues have   *but holds the*
         talked to me about similar problems   *line.*
         and how they've dealt with them.
         I think it's definitely doable.

Vince: How are we going to meet the deadlines
         that you've set?

Chris: I think we need to look at the work and
         the way it's distributed and identify
         what's getting in the way. Often the
         personality clashes are caused by some
         of the underlying structural processes.   *By openly*
         We need to have a look at what we're   *sharing her*
         doing, how we're doing it and what   *thinking, Chris*
         changes we can make. That's why I'm   *builds trust.*
         interested in the way your old team
         used to work, because I suspect you
         could share some structural process
         benefits with us.

Vince: Look, it feels like too little too late, but I guess it could work if we can be realistic about incorporating this in terms of time. Is this just another thing that we have to do on top of everything else?

Chris: I think it would be an investment of time, but I'm taking a longer-term view here. As you've pointed out, things need to change. The team's not working the way it needs to, and sometimes to move forward, you've got to take a step back. That's probably what we need to do. Maybe the Agile approach is part of the solution.

Vince: I think so. I've just felt out on a limb with this team. I hate missing deadlines and I was so embarrassed when we did. I should've contacted you. I really want this team to succeed.

Vince begins to open up here.

Chris: I want the team to succeed too, and I want you to be a part of that. I want you to feel that you're valued and respected. Let's set up a schedule, so we catch up more regularly. Would it work for you if we set up a fortnightly catch-up?

Chris provides nice reinforcement of key messages.

Vince: That would be good. I need help on the some of the specifics. Tell me, when Julie comes in and is badmouthing you, what do you want me to do?

Chris: I think we need to spell out how we want to behave as a group, and that will be part of the work we'll do with the external facilitator. Some of the behaviour that you've described today is not what we want. We all need to look at what we do want, spell that out and hold each other to account moving forward.

By acknowledging the issue and sharing thoughts on a possible solution, Chris deepens the connection.

Vince: I'm feeling a bit more optimistic, to be honest. This conversation has helped me to feel like there's a possibility of really nailing this. Thanks.

Chris: I'll get my assistant to set up a meeting in two weeks. Do Friday mornings work for you?

Vince: Friday morning would be good.

Chris: Okay – I'll send an invite. Thanks for your time. I appreciate it. I want you to walk out of here recognising that I value what you've got to contribute. I'm committed to rebuilding the team to take us to a better place.

Telling someone you appreciate their time always helps build the relationship.

Vince: Thanks, Chris. I appreciate your support.

Chris: Okay, thanks a lot.

Coaching checklist

After having a hard conversation, use the following checklist to reflect on how you managed the conversation, and what you could do differently next time.

Behaviour/ action	Descriptor	Reflections/ observations
Opening	Set up the conversation well. Spelt out the issue in a way that facilitated discussion rather than creating increased tension or defensiveness.	
Observation of the situation	Shared observations in relation to the situation (sensory data, things seen/ heard, etc.).	
Listened attentively	Listened attentively to the other person. Acknowledged what the other person was saying. Invited them to expand on what they were saying. Summarised well to demonstrate they understood what had been said.	
Open questions	Asked good 'open' questions using 'What, When, How, Who' to facilitate discussion. These questions resulted in the sharing of useful information and the questioner having a greater insight and understanding of the other person's perspective.	
Wants/ motivations	Communicated wants – for the organisation, the other person, themselves and other stakeholders.	
Actions (past/ present/ future)	Acknowledged past and present actions and recognised the possible impact these actions may have had on the other person and the situation at hand.	
Explored solutions	Discussed solutions for dealing with the issues. Considered options for moving forward having regard to mutual wants.	
Agreement	Agreed on next steps. Discussed likely obstacles and how to deal with them. Parties left with a clear understanding of who was doing what and when they were going to do it.	

Key points

- You can never confidently predict how a hard conversation will go, but you can increase the odds of it going well by preparing thoroughly using the framework outlined in this book.

- In both these case studies, issues were raised that were not anticipated. Yet the manager was able to use her skills by listening, acknowledging and exploring to gain greater understanding.

- The manager was able to address the issues raised and effectively communicate her wants and key messages to reach agreement on action to move forward.

- Having successful hard conversations relies on both good preparation and the ability to stay calm and use your skills in the moment.

Action for right now

Think about a hard conversation you've had in the past few weeks. What could you have done to have made it better? Take a look at the coaching checklist provided and reflect on what you did well and what you might have done better.

When you have a hard conversation coming up, share your preparation with a friend or colleague and role-play the situation. Then do a debrief using the coaching checklist to discuss what you might do better.

CHAPTER 7

──

Giving and receiving feedback

Giving and receiving feedback is an everyday application of the hard conversation. Often, giving or receiving feedback – even quite mild negative feedback – feels uncomfortable. This book provides you with a framework to help make hard conversations easier. You can get through the preparation – either mentally or by jotting down some notes – using the earlier framework. In this chapter, I drill into some of the nuances of giving and receiving feedback effectively while having those hard conversations.

In my workshops, I ask people to rate how comfortable they are giving and receiving feedback on a scale of one to ten – with one being hopeless and ten being fantastic. Most people are comfortable giving positive feedback. They often give themselves a score of eight or nine in this aspect. Giving positive feedback is easy. People like it and respond well.

But giving negative feedback is another story. Usually lots of fours and fives come up in people's ratings in this area. For all the reasons I discuss in chapter 1, giving negative feedback is more difficult.

People rarely like what they hear and often go into fight/flight mode, which makes you feel uncomfortable and the conversation challenging.

Receiving negative feedback is often harder still, because it goes to the heart of your identity and is often inconsistent with how you see yourself – as a capable person. Comfort ratings of two and three out of ten are common for most people in this area.

If you can become comfortable and skilled at giving and receiving feedback, individual performance improves, relationships flourish and organisations prosper. In contrast, if you give or receive feedback poorly, individual performances suffer, relationships are strained and organisations fail to achieve their potential.[1]

In this chapter, I explore:

- when to give feedback
- how to give feedback
- how to get better at receiving feedback
- how to make it easier for people to give you feedback.

Improving your effectiveness at giving and receiving feedback not only makes your life easier but also improves the way people see you as a leader.

KNOWING WHEN TO GIVE FEEDBACK

Let's start by defining feedback. In 'The power of feedback', professors John Hattie and Helen Timperley outline that feedback is information provided by one person about aspects of another's performance or understanding. The aim of providing feedback is to reduce discrepancies between current understanding or performance and a desired goal.

When and how you give feedback is important. The research suggests that giving feedback can have both positive and negative outcomes. In their article 'Feedback interventions', which outlines an extensive meta-analysis of 131 studies on feedback effectiveness, Professors Avraham Kluger and Angelo DeNisi found that while feedback interventions improved performance on average, in more than a third of the cases, providing feedback hurt subsequent performance.

Giving feedback at the right time can help create a best-practice organisation. It helps people learn and grow, drives continuous improvement, and builds relationships and trust. However, giving feedback at the wrong time can do more harm than good. You can damage the relationship and cause confusion. People may not understand the feedback, or may not be ready to hear what you have to say.

Think about your own experience. No doubt not every piece of feedback you've received has been appropriate or useful. On many occasions, you've probably walked away from receiving feedback thinking, *Thanks for nothing* or *What a load of rubbish*. But sometimes, the timing and delivery of the feedback has no doubt been useful. You were ready to receive the feedback and could absorb what was being said. And as a result, you've grown or improved.

So when should you give feedback? Giving feedback makes sense in six circumstances.

When feedback will make a difference

Remember that feedback is essentially about reducing the gap between current performance and a desired goal. If the feedback you are proposing to provide will reinforce good practice or help to improve a person's skill or approach to a task, giving the feedback makes sense. However, if the feedback you provide has no meaningful impact on improving performance or closing the gap between what is happening and what you would like to happen, don't bother wasting your time.

For example, if you were to provide me with feedback on the way I craft my sentences to improve readability, that's wonderful. Feedback that you don't like my writing style, however, will not help me improve the product.

Some feedback has the most impact if given at the time you observe the behaviour in question. For example, if you see someone is performing a process incorrectly, providing the feedback at the time makes sense. It will be easier for them to absorb what you have to say. Other types of feedback will have a greater impact if you reflect on what you wish to say and prepare for the conversation. Most of the hard conversations outlined in chapter 1 fall into this category.

When a failure to give feedback puts people at risk

If someone is putting other people at risk, it almost always makes sense to provide them with feedback in the moment. For example, if you were working on an emergency crew in a bushfire and someone is doing something that will put the lives of the rest of the crew or the public at risk, it is imperative that you speak up immediately and provide feedback to correct the behaviour.

When the person expects to receive feedback

People attend performance reviews expecting to receive feedback, so providing feedback in these circumstances makes sense. This might sound obvious, but you would not believe how many clients tell me they receive little meaningful feedback in their performance reviews.

When the person can process the feedback

Providing someone with feedback if they cannot process it is pointless. If someone is visibly upset, for example, the time is not right for feedback. You need to wait until they can process the information you wish to impart before sharing your perspective.

If you're in the middle of giving someone feedback and they have a complete meltdown, it makes sense to reschedule the meeting if you want them to absorb what you have to say.

When you are in shape to deliver the feedback effectively

Similar to the previous point, giving feedback if you are emotional is not advisable. Too many feedback conversations go pear-shaped because the person giving the feedback is upset or otherwise in a heightened emotional state. If you're not feeling calm and prepared, it's not time to give the feedback.

When you are a leader

If you're trying to create a high-performing culture, giving feedback regularly should be part of the way you work. No surprises should pop up at formal performance appraisals because you've provided meaningful feedback on performance consistently throughout the year. While you can do this informally, it's always useful to make the time in your formal one-on-one meetings to provide meaningful feedback (both positive and critical).

Ray Dalio, the founder of Bridgewater Associates, an extraordinarily successful global hedge fund, argues that giving and receiving feedback should be a non-negotiable part of the workplace culture. At Bridgewater, they encourage everyone to provide each other with brutally honest feedback all the time. Dalio calls this 'radical transparency' or 'radical candour'.[2]

A big part of the success of radical candour at Bridgewater is that they encourage it from the top down. Dalio walks the talk and encourages people to review and critique his performance. His fundamental premise is feedback is being offered with good intent – to help people improve.

In my experience, few CEOs are as comfortable as Dalio in receiving critical feedback. Few organisations have a culture where feedback is, in practice, actively encouraged. (Lots of organisations talk about it, but few do it.) While radical candour may be extreme (about a third of Bridgewater's new hires leave in the first 18 months) the underlying idea that leaders should provide regular feedback makes sense.

UNDERSTANDING HOW TO GIVE EFFECTIVE FEEDBACK

Research clarifies that while effective feedback can be powerful in enhancing learning outcomes, poorly delivered feedback leads to disengaged employees. When I talk to my coaching clients and workshop participants about feedback, they are quick to note that a vast difference exists between effective and ineffective feedback. They suggest that most of the feedback they receive does not help them. This is consistent with Gallup research that found only

26 per cent of employees strongly agree that the feedback they receive helps them do better work.[3]

So how do you ensure you give effective feedback?

I explore this question with participants in my Mastering Hard Conversations workshops. I ask them to work in pairs, sharing their positive and negative experiences of receiving feedback. Then I ask them to work in small groups to identify the attributes of effective feedback. I've done this with hundreds of groups. Based on their feedback, my experience and some of the research, I offer six suggestions for how you can provide feedback effectively.

Ask people how they like to receive feedback

Few leaders take the bull by the horns and ask the basic question – how would you like to receive feedback? I was discussing this phenomenon with Jane Mackney, one of my clients and People and Culture Director at Aon Australia – the global insurance company. Jane made an interesting observation:

> I think that the key to providing effective feedback is having an initial conversation with the people you manage to try to understand how they like to receive feedback. I take the time to have that awkward conversation with each of my team to explore how we each like to give and receive feedback. By doing this, we give ourselves permission to have the uncomfortable conversations. It always improves the relationship, increases our willingness to give each other feedback and drives greater productivity.

Provide feedback regularly

People respond best when they are getting feedback regularly – both positive and negative. People commented that receiving regular feedback built trust. When they received negative feedback from someone who was providing feedback often, they were more willing to listen to what was being said and found it less confronting.

Be clear and specific

Program participants suggested they felt demotivated and confused when the person providing the feedback failed to explain the specifics of their concerns. They noted feedback was only effective if they understood what was being said. General feedback, such as 'the report was not at the required standard', wasn't helpful. In contrast, when directed to specific errors and shown examples of how to do things, they responded positively and improved their performance.

Be respectful in the delivery

Having a two-way conversation was important to how people received the feedback. People responded positively to feedback that was given respectfully – where the context of the situation was explained, and they were asked if they were interested in receiving feedback. (They almost always were.) When they were given a chance to ask questions and offer their thoughts, they were more comfortable taking the feedback on board.

Link the feedback to the desired outcome

In 'The power of feedback', Hattie and Timperley suggest for feedback to be effective, it must address three key questions: where am I going, how am I going and where to next? Comments from the workshop participants support this research. If you link the feedback to desired goals and focus on how to move forward, the people receiving the feedback feel more positive and responsive. Participants explained that when the person giving feedback made goals clear, and showed the purpose of the conversation was to do things better in the future, this made a big difference to how they responded.

Don't do the 'feedback sandwich'

Participants almost universally agreed that the feedback sandwich (where you provide positive, then negative, and then positive feedback) was disingenuous, annoying and ineffective. While people recognised regular balanced feedback was important, they did not like receiving inconsistent messaging. If there was an issue, they wanted to hear about it unambiguously.

The sandwich approach caused participants to think that the person giving the feedback either lacked courage or was inauthentic. Others noted that when they had tried to use this technique, the recipients often ignored the substantive negative feedback and instead focused only on the positives – not the result they wanted.

BECOMING BETTER AT RECEIVING FEEDBACK

While it's important to learn how to give feedback effectively, it's also important to learn how to receive it. If you are going to give someone feedback, you're highly likely to get a little in return. When people say, 'Sure, I'd love to hear your feedback,' and sit back and listen to what you have to say, they usually then reciprocate. They say something like, 'Thanks for that. Now here's some feedback for

MASTERING HARD CONVERSATIONS

you' – which isn't always complimentary. So if you're going to give feedback, you better learn how to receive it.

Becoming adept at receiving feedback has three major benefits. First, it helps you in staying calm. (As I discuss in chapter 4, staying calm is critical to having productive conversations.) If you react to critical feedback, the situation is likely to spiral out of control and you're unlikely to get the outcome you desire. Second, becoming good at receiving feedback will fast track your ability to learn and grow. Finally, people seeing you as being good at receiving feedback builds your reputation. People think more highly of you.

Sheila Heen, co-author of *Difficult Conversations* and *Thanks for the Feedback*, reinforces these points in her 2015 TED Talk, 'How to use others' feedback to learn and grow'. Heen notes that when people become good at soliciting and receiving feedback, including negative feedback, they 'report higher work satisfaction … adapt more quickly to new roles, and get higher performance reviews'.

Receiving feedback is often difficult, particularly if you think what's being said is rubbish. Becoming good at receiving feedback does not mean accepting everything anyone ever says. Rather, it means developing your ability to listen, suspend your reaction and consider what's being offered. You need to bring your curious mindset to the conversation, reflect on what's being said, and do with it what you will. You may accept the feedback and act on it, or you may discard it and move on. It's entirely up to you. But the key is to give it reasonable consideration.

Heen notes we are all good at rationalising why we should ignore or reject feedback. She refers to this as our ability to 'wrong spot' – to identify what's wrong with the feedback, dismiss it and move on.

According to Heen, we have three 'triggers' that drive wrong spotting. First is the truth trigger. We don't accept the truth of what is being said. We dispute the validity of the data, the accuracy of the statements and so on. Second is the relationship trigger. We react to the person who is delivering the feedback rather than the substance of the feedback itself. If you have an intense dislike or lack of trust for the person delivering the feedback, it's difficult to consider that the content might include something useful. Third is the identity trigger. Here, feedback is so inconsistent with how you like to think about yourself – who you are, what you stand for – that you can't reconcile it as being accurate or relevant. For example, when you think of yourself as an outstanding leader and someone gives you feedback that suggests otherwise, it is confronting and difficult to accept.

Becoming better at receiving feedback involves managing your willingness to wrong spot – and focusing instead on your desire to learn and grow. It's useful to recognise we all have blind spots in our construction of what is 'true', and the feedback might reveal something you don't see or are not aware of. You need to suspend certainty and explore the possibilities.

To manage your relationship trigger, you need to change the story you tell yourself about the person giving you the feedback. Try shifting your mindset from 'They're an asshole who has no idea' to one where you assume they have good intent. If you can reframe and manage your relationship trigger, you may discover something valid and useful in the feedback.

When you receive feedback that seems inconsistent with your identity (how you like to think about yourself), be curious. For example, if you think of yourself as a consensus-style leader and receive feedback that says you are quite controlling, this may be hard to take. But maybe this is a good learning. Maybe when you are under pressure you do become more controlling. Ask yourself, 'Why does the other person think the feedback is justified and reasonable?' In these circumstances, you might ask the other person, 'What am I doing or saying that's making you think I'm controlling?'

Consider past feedback you have received that was uncomfortable but valuable. Often the feedback that is most confronting is the feedback we most need to hear. As a young leader, I received 360 feedback survey results that included feedback that I had 'a strong need to be right'. This was confronting, but it was true. The feedback helped me realise I needed to back off, talk less and listen more. It made me a better manager.

MAKING IT EASIER FOR PEOPLE TO GIVE YOU FEEDBACK

Jane Mackney from Aon Australia offered a simple suggestion for increasing the willingness of people to have honest conversations about performance at work – ask them how they like to receive feedback. Sheila Heen offers an equally wonderful suggestion for making it easier for people to give you feedback – ask them for feedback. By becoming proactive and seeking feedback from the people you work with, you get dual benefits. You learn and grow, and you change the way people see you, for the better.

The research suggests that people who actively seek feedback are seen in a positive light by their peers, their customers and the people they report to. Heen suggests you should periodically ask the people you work with one question – 'What's one thing I can do differently to improve my effectiveness?'

For leaders, I recommend an embellishment to the question: 'What's one thing I can do differently as a leader to help improve the way we work?' You might ask the person you report to, 'What's one thing I can do better to improve my performance?' And you can ask your clients, 'What's one thing we can do better that would make a positive difference to the way we service your needs?' Making it easy for people to give you feedback makes sense if you are serious about improving performance.

In the next chapter, I look at what you can do when you find yourself dealing with someone who isn't interested in engaging in dialogue. Drawing on the language of Professor Robert Sutton from Stanford University, I explore how to deal with 'certifiable assholes'.

Key points

- You should give feedback in the following circumstances:
  - when the feedback will make a difference
  - when the failure to give feedback puts people at risk
  - when the person expects to receive feedback
  - when the person can process the feedback
  - when you are in shape to give feedback effectively
  - when you're a leader – in which case you should provide it regularly.
- To ensure that you give effective feedback:
  - ask people how they like to receive feedback
  - provide feedback regularly
  - be clear and specific
  - be respectful in the delivery
  - link the feedback to the desired outcome
  - don't do the feedback sandwich.
- To become better at receiving feedback, you need to reduce your willingness to 'wrong spot' and instead focus on your desire to learn and grow. To manage your truth trigger, recognise that we all have blind spots and

that the feedback might reveal something useful. To manage your relationship trigger, change the story you tell yourself about the person giving you the feedback. Assume good intent and look for the value in what they have to say. To manage your identity trigger, try to stay curious. Ask yourself, 'Why does the other person think this feedback is reasonable?'

- To make it easier for people to give you feedback, ask them, 'What's one thing I can do to improve my performance?'

Action for right now

Think about past feedback that was uncomfortable, but valuable. What did you learn from it? Often the feedback that is most confronting is the feedback we most need to hear.

Think about someone you'd like to have feedback conversations with on a regular basis. Set up a meeting to talk about how they like to receive feedback. Once you've heard from them, let them know how you like to receive feedback and ask them to outline one thing you can do better.

CHAPTER 8

───

Dealing with certifiable assholes

Sometimes you work with people who are just assholes. They lack empathy and are unreasonable. Such a person could be your boss, a colleague or a client. When you need to deal with one of these people, work becomes stressful.

I started my working life as a young lawyer in a large Australian law firm in 1987. By the time I exited corporate life to start my coaching and mediation business in 2008, I had shifted from being a lawyer to a manager and worked in several types of organisations – including a large corporate, a government agency and a family business. During this time, I worked with hundreds of people and had around 20 bosses. Most were a delight to work with. Some were more challenging, but we still worked through issues and engaged in meaningful conversations.

But one of my bosses was consistently inconsistent. I realised he was a law unto himself and, with the benefit of hindsight, a narcissist. It was always about him. He had a monstrous ego. He oscillated from charming and supportive to an absolute shocker. It was, without a doubt, the most stressful and least enjoyable period of my corporate career.

The process described in this book will help make hard conversations easier if the person you are talking to:

- can listen and empathise
- is 'reasonable'.

If you are dealing with someone who lacks empathy and is selfish, the process won't always work. When this happens, you need to consider additional approaches.

In this chapter, I explore some strategies and tactics that can help deal with these particularly challenging individuals.

CERTIFIABLE ASSHOLES

Most of us sometimes act in ways we regret. We're human. We react. On these occasions, someone might reasonably describe us as 'acting like an asshole'. But what makes someone a 'certifiable asshole'?

In his classic book *The No Asshole Rule*, Professor Robert Sutton suggests two tests for identifying certifiable assholes:

Test one: After talking to the alleged asshole, does the 'target' feel oppressed, humiliated, de-energised, or belittled by that person? In particular does the target feel worse about him or herself?

Test two: Does the alleged asshole aim his or her venom at people who are less powerful rather than those who are more powerful?

Certifiable assholes have a history of behaviour that makes people feel belittled, put down, humiliated, disrespected, oppressed and de-energised. The following sidebar expands on their typical behaviour.

Classic asshole behaviour

Typical asshole behaviour, and the motivation behind it, often includes:

- *Demeaning others:* Rolled eyes, dirty looks, sarcastic comments and emails, ridiculing, personal insults, interruptions, failing to acknowledge or say hello.

- *Displaying anger:* Raising their voice, shouting, making threats (both verbal and non-verbal), and generally being rude.

- *Sabotaging others:* Undermining, ignoring, refusing to take part in discussions, lying, being late for meetings, obstructing or resisting, gossiping and unnecessary micromanaging.

- *Controlling:* Always having to win or have the last word, micromanaging.

- *Being unreliable:* Failing to follow through on commitments.

- *Glory seeking:* Failing to acknowledge and recognise others or taking all the credit.

You shouldn't assume everyone you find difficult is a certifiable asshole, because that's just a cop out. It's an excuse to avoid doing the prep work for the hard conversation. In my experience, in most workplaces, 90 per cent of the population is reasonable. You can have effective conversations with these people, even if these conversations are hard work. But approximately 10 per cent of the population are certifiable assholes, and you need to recognise them.

They need to be recognised so you don't waste time and effort, and you change your approach when talking to them.

Bill Eddy is the co-founder and Chief Innovation Officer of the High Conflict Institute in San Diego, California, and he has spent a large part of his career focusing on how you deal with certifiable assholes. Eddy is a recognised expert in dealing with what he describes as 'high conflict individuals'– or, essentially, certifiable assholes. (In this chapter, I refer to these people as certifiable assholes, because that term resonates for me.) In his book *BIFF*, Eddy suggests that common patterns of behaviour have four key characteristics that will tip you off that you are dealing with a 'high conflict person'. These are:

1. all or nothing thinking (one person is good, another is all bad)

2. unmanaged emotions (exaggerated anger, fear, sadness – out of proportion to events)

3. extreme behaviour (including yelling, hitting, lying, spreading rumours and other impulsive actions)

4. preoccupation with blaming others (people close to them or in authority).

Eddy argues you need to understand two critical things about these problematic individuals. First, they lack self-awareness. They don't understand how they contribute to their own problems. It's always someone else's fault. Second, because they lack self-awareness, they don't see the need to change their behaviour. Giving them feedback to help them understand what they need to do differently will not get you the outcome you want.

These people don't learn from their mistakes and don't change their behaviour – because, in their minds, they don't make mistakes. Trying to get them to consider your perspective doesn't work.

However, if you recognise you are dealing with a certifiable asshole, you can change your approach and take steps to increase the prospect of having a more constructive experience.

HOW DO YOU DEAL WITH CERTIFIABLE ASSHOLES?

What do you do when you realise or suspect you're dealing with a certifiable asshole?

Thinking back on my experience of dealing with one, it didn't take too long for me to realise I was dealing with a boss who was different from anyone I'd worked with before. It wasn't like I hadn't worked with difficult people, but he was different – smug, condescending, quick to challenge and at times just nasty.

He wasn't an asshole all the time. Sometimes he was charming, clever and a joy to work with. After some meetings, I'd walk out thinking I was making too big a deal of his deficiencies – but then he'd go back to type, making condescending comments, asking smart-ass questions, and applying subtle bullying behaviour to get what he wanted.

I survived. While it wasn't a career highlight, I learnt a lot about what not to do as a leader.

As I've noted, certifiable assholes believe that their view of the world is correct, and any problems are someone else's fault. They're experts at playing the blame game, so trying to engage with them and change their thinking rarely works. You have to take a different approach.

In this section, I outline 11 suggestions to help you manage these people.[1] In putting these suggestions together, I've assumed that it's safe for you to engage with the other person. If you don't feel safe, you need to disengage and find an exit plan.

These tips will help you reduce the level of stress that comes with having to deal a certifiable asshole. They may also increase the prospect of getting the outcome you desire.

Understand what you are dealing with

The starting point is to recognise the other person isn't 'reasonable', and you won't be able to communicate with them in a rationale and reasonable way. Their behaviour shows that the issues they may raise are not really the 'issues' – rather, the 'issue' is them. Bill Eddy suggests that when dealing with high-conflict people, your initial goal is to engage with them in such a way that you contain their emotions so you can try to work with them. The goal is not to convince them you are right.

Keep your composure

I talk about how important it is to keep your composure in chapter 3, but it's difficult to stay calm when someone is screaming at you or otherwise behaving unreasonably. Yet, this is what you must do when dealing with certifiable assholes. Don't take it personally – it is all about them. Treat the situation as a challenge. Breathe and use all your skills to get the outcome you desire.

Stay positive

As you grapple with the best way to deal with the situation, try to stay positive. Think about small steps you can take to make the situation tolerable. Think about the long-term benefits that await you in the future if you survive this temporary discomfort. Or think about what you can learn from working with such a dysfunctional individual. You can learn as much from your bad bosses or colleagues as your good ones.

Be clear about your goals and options

When you are dealing with a difficult person who holds a position of power, step back and reflect on your goals and options available in the situation. How committed to the organisation are you? Do you have alternative roles you can go to? What alliances do you have that might assist you? Can you tough it out? Can you reduce contact with the person? How can you leverage such resources as the People and Culture team or the Employee Assistance Program? Can you do anything else? Are there actions to make the situation tolerable, or do you need to leave?

Be brief, informative, friendly and firm

Bill Eddy suggests that when you are dealing with high-conflict people, you need to be brief, informative, firm and friendly (BIFF):

- *Brief:* Recognise that less is more. Limit the oxygen you give by keeping your responses short. This will reduce the opportunity for the other person to get triggered and go into blame mode. Instead focus on providing problem-solving information. The fewer words you give them the better.

- *Informative:* Providing objective, factual information (rather than opinion) reduces the scope for reactivity.

- *Friendly:* Being friendly can be tough when you are dealing with a really difficult person, but Eddy highlights the value of keeping things on a positive, even keel. He suggests starting the conversation by saying things like, 'Thanks for telling me your opinion on this subject' or 'I appreciate your concerns on this. Please let me give you some information you may not have …'

- *Firm:* While being friendly is important, so too is being firm and setting limits. This can be delicate, but you need to show there are limits in terms of what you will talk about, when you will talk about it and what sort of behaviour you will tolerate.

An example of a BIFF response

To illustrate a BIFF response, I here share an example of an email written by a friend of mine who runs an art school. She had received complaints from several students about the behaviour of an older student who had been making inappropriate comments to the model and other students in class. These were not the first complaints about this student. After speaking to the student to get his side of the story and pointing out the problem, she received an email from him insisting that he be allowed to stay. He stated it would be unfair to kick him out, and that he had done nothing wrong. Further, he said, if she kicked him out, he wanted a full refund.

This was her BIFF response:

Dear Graham

Thank you for your email.

I have reviewed your comments and reflected on the various complaints and our conversation last Wednesday. I have decided that it is best for the school if you continue your art education at another institution.

I will refund 50% of your fees for the balance of term 4. I note you have already had the benefit of more than 60% of your classes.

I wish you well in your future art activities and thank you for your past patronage.

Brief, informative, friendly and firm.

Adopt a 'strategic appeasement' approach

I've had a few experiences where it wasn't obvious I was dealing with a narcissist. At first, I tried to influence the other person with brilliant arguments. This got me nowhere fast. Only after I adopted a 'strategic appeasement' approach and pandered to the egos did they listen to me.

Strategic appeasement is where you seek to placate the powerful person.[2] It's important to show that you are listening and care about what they are saying, and to acknowledge the impact a situation may have on them. Even if you disagree, the key is for them to feel respected and heard, so they have a sense you are working with them, not against them. In *BIFF*, Bill Eddy also talks about the importance of using statements that show empathy, attention and respect.

This strategy allows you to build the relationship and increase your influence. It also often reduces stress and gives you time to consider your other options.

An interesting example of strategic appeasement took place during the 2020 US election campaign. Jonathan Swan is a respected Australian journalist based in the US. For many years, Swan followed and reported on the career of Donald Trump. He recognised the intrinsic nature of Trump's persona and adopted a firm but respectful approach with him when he became President. This resulted in him gaining Trump's trust and being granted a high-profile television interview with Trump in 2020, prior to the US election.

The interview was fascinating to watch. Swan listened respectfully. He complimented Trump on his achievements. Trump lapped it up. By pandering to Trump's ego, Swan created the opportunity to ask Trump some hard questions about COVID-19, which Trump tried to answer and then came unstuck. The interview, which went viral and damaged Trump, was a classic example of strategic appeasement.

In contrast, in an interview with the US *60 Minutes* just before the 2020 US election, Trump stormed off the set. The interviewer, Lesley Stahl, had taken a much firmer (though not unreasonable) approach to the interview. Uncomfortable with being challenged from the outset, Trump took his bat and ball and went home half-way through the interview. This very different approach created a very different outcome.

Appeal to their 'core drivers' to gain cooperation

I cover perspective taking in chapter 3, and appealing to the other person's core drivers is an application of this. By linking a request to your boss's or colleague's core drivers, you can often shift resistance. For example, if your boss is cost-sensitive, you might highlight that the boss's proposed solution is more costly than the boss thinks, or that a different approach would be even more frugal. The key is to understand where they are coming from to build cooperation.

Tapping into the other person's desire to look good and be a 'team player' can also be useful. By appealing to their need to be seen as delivering team or organisational outcomes, which makes them look good, you can often get a powerful difficult person to listen to what you have to say and change their approach.

Minimise contact

You may recall in chapter 2 I talk about destructive behaviours, noting that a pattern of avoidance during conflict often fails to serve you well. When you are dealing with a certifiable asshole, however, playing the avoidance card may be smart.

Minimising contact with the difficult person may be the best thing you can do. As Coleman and Ferguson argue in *Making Conflict Work*, it can make perfect sense to 'elicit less scrutiny by disappearing or appearing to be in complete compliance with demands.' I recall this was a standard practice among my colleagues in a leadership team when we had a cantankerous CEO.

Create alliances

Creating alliances is a good long-term strategy. I have a friend on a leadership team who was grappling with how to deal with a very difficult CEO. Having exhausted his arsenal of best-practice negotiation and influencing skills, he resorted to leveraging his relationship with the chair of the board. He briefed the chair on the risk to the business related to the CEO's behaviour and sought guidance on how might they move forward. By appealing to some of the core drivers of the chair (who wanted a successful business), he gained help in managing an otherwise unmanageable CEO.

By building networks, you can enhance your power and ability to influence, or at least survive, a difficult person. Because the difficult person often only shifts position in response to positional power, you may need to seek help from strong allies to help you. If you don't have a decent network, this won't be an option.

Play hardball

Sometimes you just have to play hardball. When you are managing someone who fits the description of certifiable asshole, you may need to recognise that your best approach is to leverage your positional power. If you are a consensus-style manager, this may be uncomfortable, but it may be your best option.

For example, you can remind the individual that they are reporting to you, that the organisation expects them to follow your direct requests and that if they cannot do that, you will escalate the issue to your boss.

Be conscious of your limits – your wellbeing is important

While it's fine to say, 'stay positive', you need to recognise when staying in the situation is putting your personal health and wellbeing at risk. Sometimes you just need to cut and run. Doing this is not a cop-out; rather, it's a sensible course of action.

If your organisation is going to tolerate inappropriate behaviour and you find yourself trapped working with a certifiable asshole, your best alternative may be to plan your exit strategy.

Key points

- Sometimes you will work with people who are certifiable assholes. They are not interested in engaging in dialogue. They lack empathy and are, on any objective analysis, unreasonable. In these situations, the model and approach recommended in this book won't work.

- When you have to work with a certifiable asshole, the following strategies and tactics can help you survive, reduce stress and buy yourself time to determine whether you stay or go:

    1. Understand what you are dealing with – they are the problem, not you.

    2. Keep your composure.

    3. Stay positive.

    4. Be clear about your goals and options.

    5. Be BIFF (brief, informative, friendly and firm).

6. Adopt a strategic appeasement approach.

7. Appeal to their core drivers and values to gain cooperation.

8. Minimise contact.

9. Create and leverage alliances.

10. Play hardball.

11. Be conscious of your limits – your wellbeing is important.

Action for right now

Think about a time you or someone you are close to had to work with a certifiable asshole. Review the 11 suggested strategies in this chapter and consider what you or they might have done differently to get a better outcome.

CONCLUSION

Conflict is inevitable

As you progress through your career, you will discover that the more senior you get, the more challenging conversations come your way. It's part of the gig. The good news is that it is relatively easy to improve your communication and conflict-management skills. You just need the courage to make a start. You need to push through the emotional discomfort that often accompanies conflict.

By following the simple approach outlined in this book and practising your skills daily, you will become more confident and capable of having hard conversations.

WHAT DO YOU NEED TO DO?

As a reminder, the following summarises the process outlined in this book to help you be the leader you want to be.

Recognise the benefits of having uncomfortable conversations

In chapter 1, I talk about why we avoid having hard conversations, and outline the real benefits that come from pushing through the discomfort zone. By talking rather than holding back, you can resolve problems, reduce stress, save money and increase productivity. And you build your reputation as a leader.

Instead of saying, 'I can't afford the time,' ask yourself, 'Can I afford not to?'

Increase your self-awareness

Chapter 2 highlights the importance of taking the time to assess how you are currently dealing with conflict. Understand what you're doing well and what opportunities you have for improvement.

Prepare properly – follow the preparation process

As I discuss in detail in chapter 3, you also need to invest time in preparing for the hard conversation. Don't just wing it. This preparation will be time well spent. Ask, 'What's going on for me in this situation?' Be conscious of your sensory data, your thoughts, feelings and motivations. Acknowledge how you've contributed to the situation by your actions or your failure to act.

Next, put yourself in the other person's shoes. Think about their perspective in terms of data, thoughts, feelings and motivations. Ask yourself, 'Why do they think they are being reasonable?'

Identify the open questions you'd like to ask to increase or clarify your understanding. Look for common ground. Anticipate objections and tough questions. Think about how you can best respond. What responses will keep the conversation on track?

Be clear about your goals for the conversation and your key messages. Don't have the conversation if you are not crystal clear about what you are trying to achieve.

Skip back to chapter 5 for two case studies on how this preparation process might play out.

Practise developing your hard conversation skills

As I outline in chapter 4, you can recognise that it's easy to improve your performance as a leader if you focus on improving some core skills:

- staying calm – remember to breathe
- self-reflecting
- perspective taking
- listening attentively
- asking open questions
- speaking with clarity.

Know how to give and receive feedback

In chapter 7, I run through the importance of knowing when and how to give and receive feedback, offering the following tips:

- *Make your feedback effective:* When it makes sense to give someone feedback, make sure you do so effectively. Ask people how they like to receive feedback. Provide meaningful feedback regularly. Be clear and specific. Be respectful in the delivery. Link the feedback to the desired outcome. Don't do the feedback sandwich!

- *Be proactive about leveraging the feedback you receive:* Be conscious of your 'wrong spotting' triggers ('It's not true, what would they know?', for example, or 'That's not me'.) Bring a sense of curiosity to your conversations. Recognise most feedback is provided with good intent and has the potential to help you learn and grow. And remember – while you don't have to accept feedback, it's smart to take time to contemplate it before you dismiss it.

* *Make it easy for people to give you feedback:* Periodically ask people, 'What's one thing I can improve on?'

Recognise when you are dealing with a 'certifiable arsehole'

Finally, in chapter 8 I acknowledge that sometimes you meet people who just have no interest in listening to what you have to say, or simply lack the ability to empathise. Such behaviour qualifies them for Robert Sutton's description of 'certifiable assholes'. When dealing with these people, some of the assumptions in this book don't apply and you need to change your approach. Flick back to chapter 8 for some suggestions on what you can do.

ADDRESSING BARRIERS

Many people say, 'I'm just not good with conflict.' This is a self-fulfilling prophecy. If you tell yourself you're no good, you will then either avoid the issue or deal with it badly, because you haven't taken the time to learn what you should do and practise how to do it.

As a busy leader, you're time-poor and may tell yourself, 'I don't have time for this crap.' But for many hard conversations, it makes sense to step back, do the preparation and get on with it. You will often address and resolve the issue. Effective dialogue not only solves problems, but also builds relationships and drives results.

The research on becoming highly proficient in any activity is clear – learn what you are supposed to do and then practise, practise, practise. You might never get up to the 10,000 hours required to be an expert, but any time spent practising helps!

Having hard conversations effectively is an eminently learnable skill. This book provides you with an insight into what you need to master this leadership challenge, and you will have plenty of opportunity to practise! Don't expect too much too soon. Be patient and keep plugging away.

I hope you've found what I've had to say useful. If you have any thoughts you'd like to share on this book, I'd love to hear from you. You can reach me via email at mark@balancedcurve.com. If you need help, you know where to find me.

I wish that every leader on the planet could become more skilled and comfortable dealing with different perspectives and navigating conflict. I suspect that if we can achieve this, not only would workplaces be happier and more productive, but the world would also be a better place.

APPENDIX A

Words describing emotions commonly experienced in conflict

Angry	Disgusted	Insulted
Annoyed	Distressed	Irritated
Anxious	Disturbed	Jealous
Ashamed	Embarrassed	Manipulated
Bitter	Fearful	Misunderstood
Belittled	Flat	Neglected
Bullied	Frustrated	Nervous
Cautious	Furious	Overwhelmed
Comfortable	Guilty	Perplexed
Concerned	Helpless	Pressured
Confused	Hopeful	Puzzled
Deflated	Humiliated	Rejected
Depressed	Hurt	Sad
Disappointed	Indignant	Scared

Shocked	Tired	Upset
Stressed	Unappreciated	Vulnerable
Surprised	Uncomfortable	Worried
Threatened	Unhappy	

APPENDIX B

Preparing for a hard conversation

THE PROCESS -

STEP 1
Self-reflection

STEP 2
Perspective Taking

STEP 3
Open Questions

STEP 4
Common Ground

STEP 5
Anticipating Objections

STEP 6
Clarifying Goals/Messages

PREPARING FOR A HARD CONVERSATION

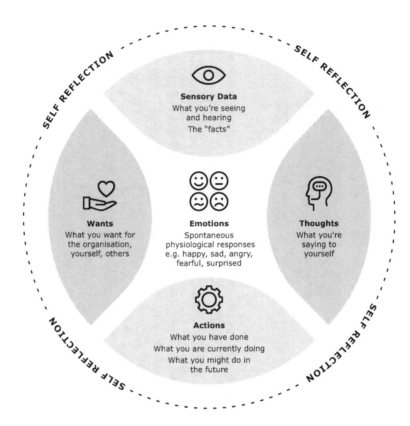

STEP 1 -
Self-reflection

Actions

_____
_____
_____
_____
_____
_____

What's going on
for you?
Briefly describe the
issue/situation.

Sensory Data

_____
_____
_____
_____
_____
_____

Wants

_____
_____
_____
_____
_____
_____

Emotions

_____
_____
_____
_____
_____
_____

Thoughts

_____
_____
_____
_____
_____
_____

STEP 2 -
Perspective Taking

Actions
_____
_____
_____
_____
_____
_____

What's going on
for them?
Briefly describe the
issue/situation.

Sensory Data
_____
_____
_____
_____
_____
_____

Wants
_____
_____
_____
_____
_____
_____
_____

Emotions
_____
_____
_____
_____
_____
_____

Thoughts
_____
_____
_____
_____
_____
_____
_____

STEP 3 -
Open Questions

What 'open' questions might you ask to gain a greater understanding of how the other person sees the situation?

_____

_____

_____

_____

_____

_____

_____

_____

_____

STEP 4 -
Common Ground

What do you both want?

_____

_____

_____

STEP 5 -
Anticipating Objections

Consider what are the objections the other person may raise in the conversation, and how might you deal with them?

Objection	Response

STEP 6 -
Clarifying Goals/Messages

What are the key goals you have for the conversation?

_____
_____
_____
_____
_____
_____
_____
_____
_____
_____
_____
_____
_____
_____
_____
_____

What are the 5-7 key messages you want to weave into the conversation?

_____
_____
_____
_____
_____
_____
_____
_____
_____
_____
_____
_____
_____
_____
_____
_____

Endnotes

Introduction

1 Kirton's work is outlined in detail in his 2003 book *Adaption-Innovation: In the Context of Diversity and Change.*

Chapter 1

1 For further detail of the model, see *Managing Differences*, pages 13–21.

2 See, for example, Thomas, KW and Schmidt, WH (1976), 'A survey of managerial interests with respect to conflict', *Academy of Management Journal*, Vol 19, No 2.

3 See, for example, Spector, PE, Bruk-Lee, V (2008), 'Conflict, health, and well-being' in De Dreu, CKW and Gelfand, MJ (eds), *The Psychology of Conflict and Conflict Management in Organizations.*

Chapter 2

1 Compare, for example, the Thomas-Kilmann Instrument (Kenneth Thomas & Ralph Kilmann, 1974), the Negotiating Styles Profile (Rollin Glaser & Christine Glaser, 1996) and Rahim Organizational Conflict Inventories (M Afzalur Rahim, 1983), which all focus on conflict styles. Conflict style instruments inevitably combine personality, motivation and behaviour to give you your style. They are defined in terms of ultimate goals such as avoidance, accommodation, compromise, collaboration and competition. This is in contrast to the CDP, which is explicitly based on behavioural orientation.

2 Feel free to contact me via mark@balancedcurve.com if you need assistance.

3 See Noble, C (2012), *Conflict Management Coaching: The CINERGY™ Model*.

Chapter 3

1 I am grateful to Craig Runde, Tim Flanagan and Sherod Miller. See *Becoming a Conflict Competent Leader* (Runde and Flanagan, 2006) and the 'Becoming Conflict Competent' course (developed by Miller, Runde and Flanagan, 2010). I also acknowledge the wonderful work of Douglas Stone, Bruce Patton and Sheila Heen in *Difficult Conversations* (1999), and Kerry Patterson, Joseph Grenny, Ron McMillan and Al Switzler in *Crucial Conversations* (2002).

2 See Miller, S, Miller, P, Nunnally, EW and Wackman, DB (1991), *Talking and Listening Together: Couple Communication*.

Chapter 4

1 Davis, DM, Hayes, JA (2011), 'What are the benefits of mind-fulness? A practice review of psychotherapy-related research', *Psychotherapy*, Vol. 48, No. 2, 198–208.

2 See, for example, Ekman, P (2003), *Emotions Revealed*; Creswell, J, Way, B, Eisenberger, N and Lieberman, M (2007), 'Neural correlates of dispositional mindfulness during affect labeling', *Psychomatic Medicine*, Vol. 69, No. 6, 560–565; Lieberman, M, Eisenberger, N, Crockett, M, Tom, S, Pfeifer, J and Way, B (2007), 'Putting Feelings Into Words', *Journal of Psychological Science*, Vol 18, Issue 5, 421–428.

3 See, for example, Hawkins, J and Blakeslee, S (2004), *On Intelligence*.

4 See Schwartz, J and Beyette, B (1996), *Brain Lock: Free Yourself from Obsessive-Compulsive Behaviour*.

5 If you want to listen to skilled, empathic listeners on radio, check out Richard Glover on 'Drive' or Richard Fidler and Sarah Kanowski on 'Conversations', both on the Australian Broadcasting Corporation. For Richard Glover, go to www.abc.net.au/radio/sydney/programs/drive; for Richard Fidler and Sarah Kanowski, go to www.abc.net.au/radio/programs/conversations/. (Richard Glover has also been featured on 'Conversations'.)

6 This questionnaire was derived from an earlier version developed by the Centre for Conflict Dynamics at Eckerd College.

Chapter 7

1 See, for example, Kluger, AN and DeNisi, A (1998), 'Feedback interventions: Toward the understanding of a double-edged sword', *Current Directions in Psychological Science*, Vol. 7, No. 3, 67–72; Hattie J, Timperley, H (2007), 'The power of feed-back', *Review of Educational Research*, Vol. 77, No. 1, 81–112.

2   For more on Dalio's views, see organisational psychologist Adam Grant's podcast interview with Dalio, 'How to love criticism', season 1, episode 1 (www.adamgrant.net/podcast/).

3   See, for example, Wigert, B and Dvorak, N (2019), 'Feedback is not enough', www.gallup.com/workplace/257582/feedback-not-enough.aspx; Brower, C and Dvorak, N (2019), 'Why employees are fed up with feedback', www.gallup.com/workplace/267251/why-employees-fed-feedback.aspx.

Chapter 8

1   I have drawn on my own experience and that of other writers in creating these suggestions. See, for example, Eddy, B and DiStefano, G (2015), *It's All Your Fault at Work: Managing Narcissists and Other High Conflict People*; Sutton, R (2007), *The No Asshole Rule*; Coleman, P and Ferguson, R (2014), *Making Conflict Work*.

2   For a fuller examination of strategic appeasement see Coleman, P and Ferguson, R (2014), *Making Conflict Work*, chapter 7.